A ROOM FOR ROMEO BRASS

Paul Fraser and Shane Meadows

A ROOM FOR ROMEO BRASS
Paul Fraser and Shane Meadows

The Original Shooting Script

ScreenPress Facsimile Editions

First published in 2000
by ScreenPress Books
8 Queen Street
Southwold
Suffolk
IP18 6EQ

Printed in England by St Edmudsbury Press

A CIP record for this book is available from the British Library

ISBN 1 901680 45 2

For more information on *ScreenPress Facsimile Editions*, screenplays and film books, contact the publishers at:

ScreenPress Books
8 Queen Street
Southwold
Suffolk
IP18 6EQ

fax on: 01502 725411
e-mail on: screenpressbooks@hotmail.com
website: www.screenpress.co.uk

Available in this facsimile series:

GET CARTER
Mike Hodges

ORPHANS
Peter Mulan

Contents

King
Nuggets

Introduction

A Room for Romeo Brass was born in a very strange stable. Paul Fraser and I were writing a Western because I was kicking against the feeling that people were beginning to see me as Ken Loach's nephew, Mike Leigh's cousin, working exclusively on working-class and social-realist subjects. In a lot of ways a Western was the wrong thing to do, but it did show me how far I was from what I should be doing. The reason I was making films about my own past, about things that I understood and things that were working class, was because that was where I was from and what was closest to my heart at twenty-five years old.

For the first eighteen or nineteen years of my life I lived in Uttoxeter, where I was born, in the Midlands. How can you try and jump away from that? I haven't been through all those stories yet. There will come a point, obviously, when I move away, but I'll move away on the basis of the years that have happened since I left there and I shan't do that until I'm ready. *TwentyFourSeven* is a tiny piece of that whole experience and what we actually began talking about while writing a Western was our past.

I went away with Paul Fraser to Stratford-upon-Avon. We stayed right opposite the theatre and we were there making short films. The only thing that was true about them, the only stuff that was really working, was the stuff we weren't writing. We were having a laugh while we were there, and what actually came out of it was at night we started talking about when we were kids, because me and Fraser grew up together, lived next door to each other, like the two characters in *Romeo Brass*.

Fraser became very ill when we were kids. We were playing football one day and he went to save a ball -- he was a very good goalkeeper and all the teachers were putting him forward for trials for teams. He landed funny and burst out crying, and everyone thought he was taking the piss, that he was just a mardy little kid. He wouldn't get up and some of the older lads were kicking him. Little did they know that he had broken a vertebra in his back from diving for the ball; he had a hairline crack in it, so it was a time bomb waiting to go off. Can you imagine how it seemed to the older boys? They saw a little kid dive to save a ball and then cry, and we all left him there too. I thought the same as everyone else; it was a matter of principle if he was going to continue crying. I went into town four hours later and he was still there. I realised something bad had happened, so I ran back up the road to talk to his dad and his dad came down, and Paul was off school for two years from that one thing. And lo and behold, me being the kind of kid I was, I went round to see him very infrequently, just like Romeo in the film.

And what actually came out of us being away was that I had clouded over these things with Fraser and put it into my head that I did go round and that his mum wouldn't let me in, but the truth of it was I really let him down. The fact that he forgave me... Well, we are talking about two years of someone being in a bedroom, through puberty in bed. His friend - someone he assumed to be his best friend, his next-door neighbour for his whole life - went off, hanging round with much older kids. I grew up too quickly through not having Fraser around. I looked up to the older kids. You know what it is like... I worshipped them. They had cars, and when you're thirteen or fourteen that's access to a brave new world. I forgot about Fraser, and in different ways that's really a very common experience, that passing up of your first friendship, exchanging a friend for someone new.

Fraser was born next door to me. We were lifelong friends. This story that people are going to see is personal, but at the same time what I wanted was not to create a day-by-day account of my life with Fraser but to touch on those issues that affect us all -- working class/upper class/middle class/king/queen, it doesn't matter. I feel sure that most people at some point in their lives have been physically taken over by someone who's bigger and stronger and able to control them. Friends you hang around with at that age you don't assess in the same way. If they have a car you just jump in the back and go to town and ask if they have a bottle of cider. In the same way, if someone has got £50 and will take you for a chicken meal, you jump on board and don't think about it. The film's about that - those common experiences a lot of people have. Obviously this is personal to me and Fraser and our past, but...

So we're in Stratford-upon-Avon ten years after we've left the town and we're writing a Western when we start to talk about that period of our lives, and we realise that if we leave it much longer we are both going to have forgotten, so it's something we should write now. And that's what films should be: they should drag you kicking and screaming, saying you've got to make them next.

The Western was in development - I had got a first-look deal with Company Pictures in London. I rang them one night and the producers went into this expecting basically everything/anything to happen, and this was the first of many twists and turns. The Western wasn't going fantastically well, although now when I look back at it there was potential. The producers came on board and were waiting for it to happen. From my point of view, I've always had that support from them on this film. They know the thing that makes a Shane Meadows film is to allow me to deviate and make my own mistakes and find the truth in what I'm actually doing. I've got someone to work with now who does not have their own agenda. They leave it at the door when they come in, together with everything they have learned with other people before. With me they might have come to rehearsals and thought that things looked quite bizarre, but because we had been through *TwentyFourSeven* before, they knew there was going to be an end result, even if they couldn't see it themselves, and even if I couldn't see at that particular point either.

We sat round a table with the script and asked ourselves what we were looking at financially, as that is my weak spot. I really can't look at a script and say you need $2 million or $3 million. But I knew I didn't want any less than for *TwentyFourSeven*, as I don't like underpaying the crew. I think that when people are working all the hours God sends for less than they should be paid, you run out of goodwill eventually. What came about in the end was that George [Faber] and Charlie [Pattinson], the producers, had just made *Titanic Town* for 3 million, and that had run along similar lines to this in terms of locations. The most important consideration for the funding was that with children under sixteen your whole schedule is different. With a film like this with kids they need fifteen minutes off for every hour worked. There were all these rules and stipulations, and the mad thing was that every council has its own criteria. For example, some councils allow children to be worked like slaves from dust to dawn. In Nottingham it was quite strict and at the end of the day, when we were all ready to go, the children would have to start lessons with a tutor. That was really difficult, as they had already done a day's work, so it was harder for them than for anyone else. Anyway, when we came to fund the film we had to take that into account.

TwentyFourSeven didn't make a lot at the box office, and I thought I might have to take a million or three-quarters of a million, supposing that the money you could raise for your next film was directly related to the previous film's success. I was really surprised to find that there were a number of people who were willing to put double what we had had on *TwentyFourSeven* into the next film, and then you sit back and wonder what makes them do that. It's part fear and part out of respect, because *TwentyFourSeven* did get honoured. I didn't realise that critical acclaim was so important, and because this expectation was building up around *TwentyFourSeven* nobody held it against me or the film that it didn't make zillions at the box office.

There is an almost healthy fear out there for someone like myself who is making his own personal films and directing. What you gather is that people think you will have a successful movie soon. Of course that goodwill won't last for ever and I won't be able to make fifty films that don't make any money, but you get the feeling that people don't want to miss out. This film or the following one may turn out to be a smash, and it's that that does it. Obviously the story comes into it too, so if you have a story about a guy who sells eggs it's going to be difficult to sell, but if there is a strong story there and people like what they have seen in your other work, even if all you get is critical success, you've got a chance.

It was a lot easier getting this film funded than it was *TwentyFourSeven* because all I had made at that point were short films, but once I had made a coherent feature film that came in under budget things improved. I have come in under budget twice now. The one thing that came in over budget was the soundtrack for *TwentyFourSeven*, but everyone realised that it was a very strong aspect of my work that hadn't been budgeted for early on, so in *Romeo Brass* we actually budgeted three times as much for the soundtrack. On my second film, then, I was able to sit down and know the kind of film I was making: know roughly what ratios of film stock to use, know that the soundtrack budget was a bit extreme but at the same time I'm going to be putting money into that while taking it off elsewhere, because I didn't want ridiculous gadget cameras and ridiculous film stocks that are just experimental. From that point of view it was much easier.

Early on in my career when I was trying to get funding for short films it was impossible. I set out to make a film every month. That is your aim when you are on the dole, and for every month that passes you by you sit there thinking that you're a lazy bastard, that you could have made a film. If you are driven and you find something that you want to do, you will find a way. People think that everything depends on money. Obviously money enables you to make something that looks like a film, but if there's nothing *but* money the centre and the passion will be missing. I would apply for funds and then not hear if my application had been accepted. Three months later I might hear that it had been received and that someone would be getting back to me. Then the decision would be postponed. In the end I just got pissed off and carried on making films. I was lucky enough to get a job as a volunteer in a film workshop where I was able to use the video camcorder, but at the same time if it hadn't been there I'd have gone and hired one for the weekend. And if you don't have funding, you don't have the pressure of someone saying that what you've shot bears no resemblance to what you wrote in your application. Because what you thought was a great idea might not work once you start. I have been on set with something I thought was a groovy idea and it's actually turned out to be shit, and I have stopped half-way through and decided to make a completely different story.

When it comes to your first film you can hold out for things if you have the energy. I chose all the people I wanted in *TwentyFourSeven* and stood my ground with *Romeo Brass*, because I'd been right the first time. But I also wasted a lot of time fighting when I should have trusted other people's experience. When it came to casting, I thought that was one of my strengths. I might use a star or all non-actors, but they will always be the right person for the part, though that is not to say that the people you pick are always the best on the day.

With *Romeo Brass*, what I did on was to bring people on one at a time with Paddy [Considine], because I knew him really well, and I said to him without him ever acting in anything before that he was my man to play Morell. It's not a big part in the screenplay but I felt he could make it what it has got to be, which is the catalyst for the whole film. So what happened was that Paddy, completely unpaid, came to work for me. I would sit in these sessions and I thought to myself, if someone can fight against him and get screen time off him, one of these kids against a guy who has an exceptional talent, they are my man. So Andrew [Shim], who plays Romeo, was auditioning 'Knock, Knock' against another Romeo. Romeo was meant to be the strong one in the relationship, and you can imagine Romeo trying to pull Andrew. As I set up scenarios, they were to improvise. Whoever won the improvisation had to convince the partner to go to a party, and Andrew just destroyed him. He looked at him and pulled his hand back, not to hit him but he said, 'You fucking go there, you just fuck off. Fine. I want nothing to do with it.' He was like a thirty-year-old man, and I looked at him and thought, that kid's been living without his Dad. He is now a man beyond his years.

When you are choosing cast you might go for someone who is incredible and just fits in, or you might see someone who is rough around the edges but you know you can work with over a couple of months. I would split the kids into groups on looks alone, to see who would fit into which category, and Andrew was on the borderline for being the biggest, chunkiest 'Knock, Knock', but because he had a kind face I didn't see him as Romeo. He had it, and they all seemed to have it. I was very lucky there wasn't anybody I had to work up or take a chance on. I would have taken a chance, but I couldn't believe it. I felt this was such a strong cast and within three or four weeks of casting I had assembled this massive confidence. Vicky [McClure] was chosen to be nineteen or so, but she was only fifteen. She had very little experience but she was right every time. People who were chosen did not try to steal the limelight all the time; it's equally important to sit back in a scene. But for me the people who were chosen had a subtlety as well as a strength, and literally what happened was, if you look at Romeo's family, Andrew's black, his mum's mixed race, his friends are white, Ladine's white, but you don't think about it, and you don't think about it because that is what families look like. For me, even if Andrew had been Chinese and Ladene [Hall]- Carol - had been Russian, if there's a chemistry between the people, you believe. If he believes that she is his mother and vice versa, it doesn't matter. You know if you have confidence then you will sell anything, and I was going to put people together that were those characters, so Andrew was Carol's son.

Some cast by looking for familiar characteristics with characters, but I don't care. Whatever's right for the film. I don't have actors read from the script for an audition. On set they are going to be pushed to the limits of improvisation, so I feel you should test them in a way that you will test them later on. It was those people who showed strength. On the occasions they couldn't get there with someone they were working with, they would say, 'My head's gone out of it.' I like that. It led to a very long rehearsal period -- three months -- trying to make these people feel like families.

On *TwentyFourSeven* I had a week's rehearsal time -- just seven days. I didn't know any different then, as on my other films I had not had any rehearsal time. On *TwentyFourSeven* I was told most people have a week or two and that I had one, but in a lot of ways I would have liked to take those characters and learn more about them. We did very well in a week, but at the same time with *Romeo Brass* I wanted things to be different. I wanted a massive soundtrack budget so I could use any music I wanted. I wanted complete freedom over casting and a long rehearsal period, as for my money this film was always going to be character-driven; it was never a script-oriented film. We were going to use the script as a backbone and then everything else was going to come in those rehearsals.

What happened was we would rehearse a scene that would be so much better than what we had written, and Fraser would take that down word for word and put it in the script, and then other times we went through something that we thought wasn't going to work word for word and it would be fantastic, and Fraser and I would have this melting pot again -- a real amalgamation. The actual script was made up of 30 or 40 per cent improvisation. We were man enough not to be proud and say we wanted to keep to the script. Fraser is very big really. He had worked on the scripts and then they got taken out of his hands, but what ended up happening was he would come with a camcorder and sit filming the rehearsals and would never say that his scene was better.

We were both agreed that if something worked fantastically it didn't have to be that the script was the script and the acting was the acting, and what happened was we rehearsed too much. It was the complete opposite of *TwentyFourSeven*. When we started shooting we had already rehearsed for three months. We had been rehearsing at least once a week to start with and then two or three days a week, and then two weeks on the trot. So we were overworking the script, and what I decided to do before the shoot, as we were all getting tired, was to set up situations that had nothing to do with the film. I would set up a game with Morell and all the women. I would talk to them privately, saying, 'You fancy him', 'You hate him', 'You're not sure', 'You're not sure but can be won over', 'You fancy him but pretend to dislike him.' So Morell would come in and try to schmooze these chicks and it was so funny and put energy back in. So we did a lot of games and mad quiz shows, or it might be Andrew and Ben [Marshall] sat there talking about football. We did this for the last week, so when we started working on a scene they had the energy for it. We had nearly got to the point of working it to death but hadn't.

When I started shooting we had 3 million to make the film and the script was far more wide-ranging than what happened in the rehearsals. From the rehearsals it was apparent that it needed to be set between three locations: the flat/Knock, Knock's house/Romeo's. That sounds rather boring, but when you are character-driving things, you just need it. We went in to start shooting this 3-million film, but on the basis of the rehearsals it could easily have been done for 1 million.

Because we had the money and the time, I started looking at the rushes and they were too clever. What was missing was the feeling I had had watching the rehearsals, crying with laughter in the last week. The performances were there, they weren't any different, but I was not laughing because I could feel the camera moving, and so after three days the rushes weren't right. No one else could see it, but I could feel that it was not going together, so I went back to Ashley [Rowe], the cameraman, and said this isn't going to do you any favours but I want to take the tripod and track away. I want the camera on your shoulder, not like rough and extreme, but I want it to feel how it felt for me in those rehearsals.

We started doing that and the track worked its way in when Knock, Knock is in his bedroom and the camera moves away. Those movements are beautiful, and the light coming round and touches like that were great, but we were doing it everywhere, and from my point of view when you shoot a film you should be prepared to stop the system and start again. That is the key for me. Don't think three films down the line you know everything, as you kind of know more but then there are a load of other things you thought you knew but you don't. At rehearsals those people are dropped into those front rooms and you need to capture that. You have to find a way that feels like those people live in that house. What was happening was it felt as though they were on a set, and so I was looking at the rushes and everyone was saying they are great. I knew when they were put together I didn't want the street to look rough and all on the shoulder and working class, but at the same time there was no breath in it, no life, and it was only going to become apparent later on. I was very scared, but once we had taken the tripods out and when we did shoot those moments it was special.

As a director, shooting is all about hindsight. I love finishing shooting, when you know you will be able to go into the edit suite and work on the film. I do enjoy shooting, but the stress of things going wrong... I had people flying over, doing loop-the-loops constantly, to the point that one day, when I had the flu and a fucking migraine, I was saying, 'Put me in the fucking car and take me to the airfield. I just want to go down and see him.' I wanted to go and pull this guy's teeth out, as if these people were taking the piss, and we found out it was the RAF and they were going off-course to annoy us just for the reason that they could! When you are making a film, not knowing what will go wrong next is stressful. Also when you have kids, they can only work certain hours. So you have the clock ticking and these fucking planes won't go away and the kids need to go in five minutes for a lesson and you haven't got your shots!

Editing for me is the most enjoyable part, as it's got a control that none of the other areas have. When you are in rehearsals or have started shooting you think about all the things that could go wrong. Then you land in an edit suite with a leather sofa and a fridge full of drinks... I am beginning to discover that most editors drink red wine -- when you arrive they have this 'I've just had five glasses of red wine' look and are dead chilled and mellow.

I'm obsessive while editing. When I was editing *Romeo Brass* I was living half a mile from the centre of London on the way out of Soho and at two I would wake up with an idea in my head and would walk in and get propositioned by prostitutes or offered drugs every fucking night. It was alien to me and I would say, 'I'm fine, thanks,' to the hookers and, 'No, I'm sound for that, thank you. I have got to get to work.' I would work from three or four in the morning a lot of the time, through to nine or ten, when the editor would come. I would then go to sleep for a couple of hours or I'd leave him a note. When I am editing I have this energy. You finish the shoot and you think you will take it steady and give yourself set hours to work, but it takes hold of you.

The end of the film as it is now just came. It hardly changed during the editing process. The rest of it was a mess, but I thought the end had precedence and wondered how could we get the rest of it to lead there. If I was having a real problem I would leave it to one side. As it was my second film I had learned from my mistakes on *TwentyFourSeven*. What I learned on this one was if you are not 100 per cent sure about any of it, you must do everything in your power to get it right. There were certain things on *TwentyFourSeven* that I thought would do and I then regretted it later. I can genuinely say with *Romeo Brass* I put at least 140 per cent into everything. That is not saying it is perfect, as nothing is, but if you give yourself an easy break and you just knock off and leave those things, you're not going to be a good film-maker. If you know those weaknesses are there, you have to do something about them. It is almost an insane thing, but you have to almost abuse yourself. There were times during the edit when I was doing too much, but it's the passion, the feeling that you do not want to be left with anything you didn't put your heart into, because as long as that period seems when you are editing, that two or three months and through all the sound dub, afterwards the film is with you for the rest of your life.

I think for me editing is what I am waiting for on a film, as I know I have all the material. It's in my hands and I can make something of it. Shooting can be the same to a certain extent, but the surroundings affect you so much more. With editing you can be down the darkest alley and be driving back in a taxi and you will hear a song on the radio and think, fucking hell, Nina Simone, I'm going down to the shop in the morning. And it never dies. You come back in and put Nina Simone on and suddenly it fits, and the whole fucking sequence works and you put something in front of it and suddenly the tension's there. So editing is one of those things you should never give up on.

The editing process, because *Romeo Brass* was the kind of film that was shot so broadly, was always going to be incredibly difficult. This is the time you can make, break and completely change the style. The way films are made in general is they shoot and get the rushes and the films are built after that, but I build them differently. I want every performance, every shot to have the potential to be used in its entirety, and you will notice in *Romeo Brass* that there are a lot of single shots. If something worked for me in a single shot, I didn't shoot any more. Editors may feel they need a little cover on this, but when I have a fight sequence that works in one shot then I stay there and give myself the options, because you lose it at certain points in edits and those are the times when you put things in that are not needed.

I suppose because the edit got extended by so much no one had seen anything, and I was away for months and months and had not seen those people I had been so close to. Screenings are in three or four months, and then you are back together and it's not such a gap, but what had happened was I was so far into editing it went on and on, and you can't have anxiety, so when we had the cast and crew up it felt like five years since we made the film, and you knew that everyone had been so far from the film that they were going to have a very clear and objective vision. Normally at these first screenings the actors sit there and worry about how they look, which is natural. But this screening was the best chance of having a genuine audience response, because people's lives had moved on and the film shoot was right back in the distance.

We had the screening in Nottingham and because of the nature of the film and a lot of them hadn't acted before, there were whole families there. So rather than it being for a normal cast and crew with everyone from the business who knew the score, it needed to be of a very high standard. We got a rush print of it and the response was just breathtaking. You literally suffocate in those first screenings and when people don't laugh immediately at a point you know to be funny, you are like a mad professor-editor who has created this mad fucking vision, and all these people see it after it has just been you trapped in an edit suite with one or two other people, and then you bring it back to all these people who have had so much to do with it and made it what it is. To see people like Andrew and Paddy, who have never acted before, speechless at the end and getting praise from all those people was fucking joyous.

I had been through that with *TwentyFourSeven*. The first time you start getting praise from people and you see them crying from something you have made, it just blows you away. I will never be able to recapture that, which is sad, but when you see Andrew with a group of girls around him wanting to mother him and look after him and take him home, it takes you back to when it happened to you. It doesn't matter how many films I make, if I continue to work the way I am working now I can always recapture that feeling through the people around me who are experiencing it for the first time. I don't think that feeling will ever go away if you care about the project and it takes as much out of you as *Romeo Brass* did.

I have not had a horrific experience as yet and I know it's got to happen. No film-maker on earth who has continued to work has had success with every film and I honestly don't know how I will respond if and when I have one of those goddamn awful experiences. I went to the screening with a certain amount of anxiety. A film takes over your life and each time you have to start right at the bottom with your new one. If it is shit, no one will give you credit because of what you did before. That first screening is the most difficult, as those people who are forced to trust you may sit back and see it and think, God almighty, but luckily they did not and it was fantastic.

I am not a big fan of test screenings, as the people who are there know they are there for a reason and so they watch the film in a different analytical way. They know they will be answering questions and they then judge and assess things on a different level than if they had just walked in and paid £3 and sat down. It makes the film more vulnerable.

When we finished the first couple of cuts of the film, it went to Cannes and Venice, as both were very keen to see it and were almost scrapping over it. We sent it to Cannes and didn't hear anything. It took ages and we were having to ring them. It's a horrible position, having to chase, so we had a bad feeling -- you just get a gut feeling that it won't work out. At Venice no films were being selected as yet, whereas with Cannes Mike Leigh and loads of people got turned down. What happened there was they chose all the French films. With Venice it was a much closer-run thing. We were in there, but the section we were in there were other things going on. They were favouring it over other films within the section but didn't truly love it. They liked it and it got down to us and one other film, and we fell at the last hurdle.

That does start to knock your confidence, as it was two in a row. It's not that you don't believe in your film, but you know that knock-back will reverberate. So initially we weren't in any festivals. The film then went to Edinburgh and we weren't expecting much, but within fifteen minutes of them watching it, it was in. It was a real boost, no question. They spoke about the film being my best to date. It was like an injection in the arm. I was also physically exhausted and to have the energy to go to the next stage you need a lift.

While we were at Edinburgh I chatted to Lynne Ramsay, the director of *Ratcatcher*. I respect her work. She hadn't massively liked *TwentyFourSeven* and I was interested to know what she thought about *Romeo Brass*. She was really taken with it, really enjoyed it.

So it was one of those festivals. The film took on a life of its own. From there it was taken to Toronto and it's been climbing ever since. After the first two turn-downs you can't see the light at the end of the tunnel, but it has now been accepted at Sundance and what we are actually doing is far healthier than with *TwentyFourSeven*. That started on a peak. It went straight in really high and they were saying Shane Meadows is the next Steven Spielberg, the new Martin Scorsese, and then when the film was released some months later I think it had already peaked.

We have not tested any European territories because what happened in Cannes and Venice has tainted it a little bit. But any in any of the English-speaking countries that don't need subtitles it has transferred beautifully. The last festival was London. It was very cosmo and everyone could go and could afford it. We took Andrew and Paddy. Andrew played pinball all the time and Paddy was searching for Star Wars figures, so Fraser and I hung around together. London was fantastic, though they are quite a difficult crowd to impress, but it is not a very central festival. You go to Edinburgh and you know where the festival is, it has a heart and soul, but London is spread all over the place. We managed to get an incredibly warm reception, so it's really exciting as it doesn't feel like the film has reached its peak yet, which is a nice position to be in.

You start to form relationships with festivals. Your ideals and that of the film tend to match. What you find is that the sorts of films that are rejected to begin with will always be rejected. So as long as you continue to work in the same fashion and follow the same principles I think that you find partnerships. For example, *TwentyFourSeven* was selected for Venice. We had massive success, a standing ovation, the full works -- couldn't believe it, it really knocked me of my feet. But the very next year a completely new guy took over and the relationship was over, which was sad.

On one level, festivals are there for you to sell the film. If you can create a buzz the price of the film starts to go up, and you try and find a marketplace for it. You put yourself around as a director, going on the circuit, and primarily, from my point of view, it gives you some idea of how far and wide your film will actually go. When a lot of countries want to show your film, you know you have something that will touch people all over the world.

When you make short films on video, you have a limited audience, but with movies you suddenly realise there are all these festivals. You have a chance if you make your way round the world and present yourself and your work. I'm not a fan of talking the film up before it is screened. But I might find someone I spoke to the year before will come up to me and watch the film. I might talk to twenty or thirty people at each festival from the last time, and the knock-on effect is that I am developing fans who will hopefully follow my work throughout my life.

I go and see other people's work, and even if I'm not so keen it doesn't stop me seeing their next film, as I believe in them. So going to festivals is about finding world audiences and developing relationships. I spend my time talking to people who are interested in what I do and how I work, and respecting the people who watch my films. They might be only a small percentage, but come the day when it matters and these people go and see your films, that really counts.

Shane Meadows
January 2000

A Room for Romeo Brass

A Room for Romeo Brass

Romeo Brass and Gavin 'Knock Knock' Woolley are two twelve year old boys living in a small town in the Midlands. They are next door neighbours on a housing estate . Knocks walks with a slight limp and is very small and skinny. He is waiting for an operation on the NHS. Romeo is very thick set for his age. He lives with his mum and half sister Ladine. Romeo's father left them three months ago.

1 EXT. FIELDS OVERLOOKING TRAIN TRACK. MORNING DAY 1 1

Romeo and Knocks are sat on a hill side overlooking the train track. It's around eleven o'clock, we see traffic on the road, it's a hot day. People are buzzing around outside the factory on the other side of the track. Knocks is contemplating something or other, Romeo is shooting his catapults at a log.

KNOCKS
My dad's hidden his porno mags again

ROMEO
Flippin' heck, what's that guy's problem.

KNOCKS
He knows we've been in 'em.

ROMEO
Did he go mad.

KNOCK
He can't can he. They don't exist. if me mum found out she'd throw him out.

ROMEO
What are we gonna do. I've only got that seventies one. All the women in it are dead old now.

KNOCK
I ain't bothered. They're young in the mag on't they.

ROMEO
No but there's blokes with brown pants and sideburns in every picture. It puts me right off.

KNOCKS
Just cover them over

CONTINUED

1 CONTINUED: 1

ROMEO
I just don't like the era full stop. Everyone's to hairy and old before their time. I want a new one desperately. They do all sorts now you know. Women from abroad an'all that jazz

KNOCKS
Me dad's got the lot ant'e the selfish bastard.

ROMEO
Can't we go an'ave a look.

KNOCKS
I've tried. We ain't gonna find em this time. This time he's hidden 'em for good.

Silence for a moment.

ROMEO
Train....

Both lie on the ground and raise their feet in the air - a game, it's bad luck to have your feet on the ground when a train passes. We cut to a close up of the train speeding past from the factory side. This leads us to a view of the two from a distance, both with their feet in the air. Something like 'Into the Mystic' - Van Morrison begins, along with the opening credits.

2 EXT. FRONT TITLES. MONTAGE. DAY 1 2

We go into a montage sequence of the two lads and how they spend the rest of the day. An opportunity for us to see their friendship - Very much loafing about. The sequence continues until early evening - the two walk back up the road to their houses, the credits and music conclude with both lads walking through the gates of their houses.

3 INT. ROMEO'S HOUSE KITCHEN/LOUNGE. EVENING 1 3

Romeo enters his house. He is carrying a bag of chips in a carrier bag. We follow him through to the lounge, a slow process. He dumps his bag on the kitchen table, grabs a can of pop from a fridge that contains little else. In the lounge is Romeo's mother, Carol.

CONTINUED

3 CONTINUED: 3

She's slumped on her arm chair, smoking a fag and finishing a can of cider. He sits beside her. They watch TV for a few moments.

ROMEO
You watching this..

CAROL
Nar.. Change it.

He does. He begins to take his chips out of his bag.

CAROL
(continuing)
You get me any chips..

ROMEO
No..

CAROL
I'm starvin'. Make us a chip butty out of yours Rom. they smell lovely.

ROMEO
Flippin' heck. Can't you go an' get a bag. There's hardly enough as it is. I'm starving myself.

CAROL
Who paid for 'em.

ROMEO
Ya know who paid for them.

CAROL
Well make me a butty then.

ROMEO
Oh I'll make you one alright..

Romeo storms out of the Room into the Kitchen. We cut to the sound from the next scene.

4 EXT. KNOCKS HOUSE. EVENING 1 4

We see Knocks dad pull up outside his house. The horn beeps on his car for about three seconds. He didn't do it. It keeps going off by itself. He gets out and looks very stressed.

CONTINUED

4 CONTINUED: 4

He lifts the the bonnet up on his car to try to stop it. It goes off for another bout. Bill taps this and that, it goes off again. He whacks this and that and off she goes again. He slams the bonnet shut. Turns the car off and storms of up the path.

5 INT. KNOCKS HOUSE. KITCHEN. EVENING 1 **5**

Cut to inside Kitchen. We see a shot of some eggs frying. We pull out to reveal Sandra monitoring the proceedings. Knocks is at the table. He's doing his homework.

SANDRA
How's your back been love..

KNOCKS
Not too bad..

The back door opens. Bill, the father, enters. He appears dusty from a day out in his lorry. He plonks his bag down, taps knocks on the head with his copy of the Daily Mirror, moves across to Sandra, He stands before the two.

SANDRA
You want sausage or pie..

BILL
It's happening again.

He exits.

SANDRA
What about you..

KNOCKS
I turned vegetarian this morning.

6 INT. ROMEO'S HOUSE. LOUNGE. EVENING 1 **6**

Romeo enters the Room with a small plate. On it there are two pieces of bread. At first glance one would think that it was a completely empty sandwich. But closer inspection will illuminate the one small lump somewhere towards the right rear of the sandwich.

There lies one, green, uncooked chip from the wrong side of the track.

CONTINUED

6 CONTINUED: 6

Romeo hands her the sandwich. She sits silent momentarily. Romeo does not crack. She lifts the top piece of bread. We see one very ill chip lying there in need of dialysis. Carol looks up at Romeo. Romeo looks sternly back. She bursts out laughing.

CAROL
You are unbelievable. Shove your sandwich up your arse.

7 INT. KNOCKS HOUSE. KITCHEN. EVENING 1 7

Sandra and Knocks are sat at the table, with mugs of something hot. Bill enters. He wears a towel around his waist, obviously about to jump into the bath.

BILL
(He looks very angry)
Do you mind if I interrupt.

KNOCKS
No, what is it.

BILL
Have you been in me cabinet upstairs.

There is a silence.

BILL
(continuing)
Have you been in me bus cabinet upstairs.

KNOCKS
Yes, I have.

BILL
What have I told you about going into that cabinet

The sight of a half naked Bill in a mood is too funny, Sandra and Knocks try not to laugh.

BILL
(continuing)
How's he supposed to learn any respect if you won't even take it bloody serious Sandra, ah..

CONTINUED

7 CONTINUED: 7

KNOCKS
I haven't damaged them.

BILL
You broken the seals on three of the boxes, he's changed the destination boards with letraset. Do you realise what you've done..

KNOCKS
Not really no..

BILL
It's not funny... You've devalued the whole set by thirty percent.

Sandra bursts out laughing. Bill leaves the room. Sandra shakes her head whilst looking at Knocks then sticks her fingers up at Bill's back. Half joke, half serious. Bill turns round Sandra changes her fingers to a thumb abd smiles. Bill returns and sits at the table. Sandra just stares at him. Knocks feels uncomfortable.

BILL
(continuing)
He's painted on one of um.. Blood and Custard, they dunna make um in those colours anymore..

SANDRA
Ya should lock them away if they're that precious.. Gavin say sorry..

KNOCKS
Sorry

SANDRA
There.. Ok

BILL
Well no, not really..

Sandra looks over at Knocks and signals for him to go upstairs. He gets up and leaves.

BILL
(continuing)
What's all that about..

CONTINUED

7 CONTINUED: (2) 7

SANDRA
What..

BILL
That.. 'say sorry Gavin'.

SANDRA
Bill, they're toy buses.

BILL
A can't believe you just said that, you know what they mean to me Sandra..

She gets up and leaves the room.

BILL
(continuing)
Sandra..

8 EXT. ROMEO'S HOUSE SIDE PASSAGE/PORCH ROOF. NIGHT 1 8

Evening has come upon us. We see Knocks walk along the side of Romeo's house. Rather than go to the door, he climbs onto the porch roof using a ladder, and taps on the window.

9 INT. ROMEO'S HOUSE. BEDROOM. NIGHT 1 9

We cut into Romeo's bedroom, he is sat on his bed. He's looking at the underwear section of the catalogue. He flips back to the video page when he hears the knock at his window. He opens it. Knocks climbs in.

KNOCKS
Alright.. What you looking at.

ROMEO
Viddypants... er Videos, Beta Max.

Romeo chucks down a cushion. Knocks turns and grabs a blanket from on top of the wardrobe. Romeo sticks his fingers up at him until he turns back. He lays the blanket and cushion neatly on the floor, then sits on them. He puffs up his pillow and settles down.

ROMEO
(continuing)
Turn the light off then..

CONTINUED

9 CONTINUED: 9

KNOCKS
I've just got comfy, you do it..

ROMEO
No.. you do it, or you leave.

KNOCKS
What about me back..

ROMEO
If you can climb a ladder, you can turn a light off.

Knocks tries to think of a way out of this, he can't. He turns the light out. They remain in darkness for a while.

KNOCKS
You've got a hairy ass.

ROMEO
You've got tits growin' on your back..

They both laugh.

KNOCKS
Have you read Danny the Champion of the world.

ROMEO
Yeah we did it school last year.

KNOCKS
I'd love to have a dad like that bloke.

ROMEO
I love that book you know. I've only read about three books in my entire life.I should read more books really. I enjoy reading when I actually sit down and start.

KNOCKS
Yeah I know what you mean.I'm lucky really, I always seem to choose good books somehow.

9 CONTINUED: (2) 9

ROMEO
Yeah that's true that is you know, The three I've read have all been good.

There is a pause.

ROMEO
(continuing)
Have you got a fine on your librairy card.

KNOCK
Nah.

ROMEO
We could get one of them what's it called. Karma Sutra books.

KNOCKS
There pencil drawings though an't thee.

ROMEO
There's one in there that's like a Naked yoga one. Taken from a T.V. programme. It's all colour pictures.

9A INT KNOCKS HOUSE. PARENTS' BEDROOM - MORNING 2 9A *

(Scene to be written: Bill, Sandra and Knocks) *

10 EXT/ INT. KNOCKS HOUSE. LOUNGE/FRONT DOOR/BACK GARDEN. 10 DAY 2

We cut to the next day. We see a shot of Knocks, his Mum and dad sat in their front room. All have mugs of coffee. Bill is watching TV, checking the football results with the coupon, Sandra is cleaning a replica bus. Knocks is writing, We hear a Knock at the door. Sandra looks at Bill. Bill looks at Knocks, smiles and turns back to the T.V. Knocks huffs and gets up to answer it. We cut outside. There are two young lads stood on the doorstep.

Knocks answers the door. The first young lad seems very nervous.

CONTINUED

10 CONTINUED: 10

KNOCKS
What's wrong..

CONTINUED

10 CONTINUED: 10

FIRST LAD
(Deleted)
My ball bounced of the washing line and landed in your garden.

KNOCKS
Just go an' get it..

FIRST LAD
Your dad said he'd stab the next ball that came over

KNOCKS
Go on, you'll be alright. I won't say anything.

The lad smiles and walks off sharply towards the back of the house with his friend. Just as they are clearing the shot Bill comes thundering out of the front door. Knocks is pushed out of the way. The chase begins. The lad begins running up the garden chased by Bill, desperate to confiscate the ball. They run up the path, Bill slightly behind. Fifteen feet from the ball, Bill is gaining all the time on the kid. Knocks looks on in disbelief. Bill draws level in the chase and just as they are about to reach the ball. Bill barges the young lad off the ball and into the hedge, then dives onto the ball and smothers it with his body. Knocks walks up the path towards the incident shaking his head. He puts his hand out to help the young kid out of the hedge. Bill gets to his feet smiling.

KNOCKS
(continuing)
Give him the bloody ball back Dad.

BILL
I'm sorry mate. You can't have sixteen accidents in one week. I'm gonna keep hold of it now, until you've learnt your lesson.

FIRST LAD
I'll get the police on you..

BILL
Ya definitely won't get it with manners like that.. Go on bugger off now.

FIRST LAD
Just give me my ball back.

CONTINUED

10 CONTINUED: (2) 10

BILL
No..

The lads walk off down the path, the first lad turns around.

FIRST LAD
You want locking up ya mad yank.

BILL
Go and put it in the house, Gavin

KNOCKS
You've got to be Joking.

BILL
Right then I'll burn it myself.

Bill goes back inside. Romeo calls to Knocks from his bedroom window using the wispered whistle signal. Knocks turns round.

ROMEO
Have you got em.

KNOCKS
No. He's been in all day.

ROMEO
Come on Knocks you promised.

11 INT. KNOCKS HOUSE. LOUNGE/STAIRS. DAY 2 11

We cut to inside. Bill is sat back down. Knocks walks through the lounge. He drops the ball on Bills lap and continues through to the stairs. You can hear a delicate thud of 'Motown Greats', coming from Romeo's house next door. He shuts the door a bit too hard.

BILL
Don't slam the bloody door..

12 INT. KNOCKS HOUSE. PARENTS' BEDROOM. DAY 2 12

We cut to him walking into his parents bedroom. The room is small and cluttered. The bed takes up most of the space. Cupboards pile up in front of the window.

He stands on a chair and feels above the previously mentioned cabinet, after a few seconds he pulls down two adult magazines.

13 EXT. ROMEO'S HOUSE. FRONT GARDEN. DAY 2 13

We cut to outside. Romeo is stood in the front garden of their adjoining house, he looks up at the front bedroom window.

14 INT. KNOCKS HOUSE. PARENTS' BEDROOM. DAY 2 14

We cut back to the bedroom. Knocks is struggling to get to the window without knocking ornaments off the drawers, he gets to the top, small, opening window. He navigates through the netting and opens the window. Knocks is in an awkward position and his back is hurting. He looks like giving up.

15 EXT. ROMEO'S HOUSE. FRONT GARDEN. DAY 2 15

We cut back to Romeo in his garden.

ROMEO
(Quietly)
Chuck them down. Please.

KNOCKS
(Quietly back to him)
I'll stick them under me jacket.

ROMEO
They'll see you.. Just throw them.

KNOCKS
The window isn't big enough.

ROMEO
Come on you flid, you promised.

KNOCKS
I'll put em in me school bag...

ROMEO
Go on, just friggin' throw them..

We see Knocks get his hand out the window, then pass himself one of the magazines.

16 INT. KNOCKS HOUSE. LOUNGE. DAY 2 16

We cut to the lounge. Sandra has got up and is about to turn the TV off. We see one of the magazines fly across the side of the window.

CONTINUED

16 CONTINUED: 16

SANDRA
What was that..

17 EXT. ROMEO'S HOUSE. FRONT GARDEN. DAY 2 **17**

We cut to Romeo picking the magazine up.

18 INT. KNOCKS HOUSE. PARENTS' BEDROOM. DAY 2 **18**

We then see Knocks pass himself the second magazine. Just as he lets go we cut into the bedroom, Sandra walks in.

SANDRA
.... Gavin, what you doin'..

KNOCKS
Nothin..

He jolts back, knocking ornaments. Off camera we hear Bill shout up the stairs.

BILL
Sandra....

19 EXT. ROMEO'S HOUSE. FRONT GARDEN. DAY 2 **19**

We cut to outside. The magazine wasn't stapled together, there is a snowstorm of pages from the magazine drifting down onto the garden, Romeo runs off.

20 INT. KNOCKS HOUSE. STAIRS/PARENT'S BEDROOM. DAY 2 **20**

Cut to Bill running upstairs and into the bedroom to check if Knocks has been in his Matchbox bus collection.

BILL
What's bloody go'in on. Is he in me bloody bus cupboard again.

SANDRA
He's just thrown some filthy magazines out the window to that bloody Romeo

Bills face changes to one of worry.

20 CONTINUED: 20

SANDRA
(continuing)
Where did you get them from. Come on who sold them to ya.

Knocks looks at his dad. His dad looks like his mum doesn't know about them.

KNOCKS
I found them.

BILL
Come on duck. All kids do it. At least he's showing an interest.

Sandra just glares at him. Bill get's more uncomfortable

BILL
(continuing)
A healthy interest. You know, he's not erm. Thingy me bob. Er.

SANDRA
Shut up Bill. Gavin go and get bloody ready for the hospital.

21 INT. ROMEO'S HOUSE. LOUNGE - MORNING 2 21 *

Romeo is sitting on the sofa. He has put the racy magazine inside a comic. He is sitting there smiling. He turns the pages and nods his head with satisfaction. Enter Carol. *

CAROL
What you doin'..

ROMEO
Just waiting for Knock Knocks..

CAROL
Am off out to work. There's a couple of quid on the side for ya tea alright.

ROMEO
Yer. what time you back.

CAROL
Well, I was going to go out tonight duck.

CONTINUED

21 CONTINUED: 21

ROMEO
Oh alright, whatever.

CAROL
See ya later then..

Romeo hasn't looked at her. She pauses at the door, she obviously feels guilty about something, but not enough to say anything, she pulls the door to. Romeo looks up to where she was.

22 EXT. KNOCKS HOUSE/STREET. DAY 2 22

An ambulance pulls up outside Knocks' house. Knocks and Sandra exit house. Romeo is already waiting outside his house. All three climb into the back. An old man and a man with a big bandage over his eye are already sat inside. They take a seat. The large chubby ambulance man sits next to Knocks. Bill climbs into his car behind them. As the ambulance pulls away we see and hear Bill, his horn starts as soon as he turns on his engine. He turns the engine off and climbs out - very stressed out now.

23 INT. AMBULANCE. STREET. DAY 2 23

We cut to inside the ambulance. There are already a few people in it being taken to the hospital for their various appointment. We focus on the ambulance assistant. He shouts to the driver..

AMBULANCE MAN
Alright Kev..

The vehical moves off.He starts talking to no one in particular.

AMBULANCE MAN
(continuing)
A lived in London all through me childhood, me and the boys..We never had two penny's to rub together, although my mate Alan did. I'll show ya what happened.

He takes a coin from his pocket. He holds it out between thumb and finger. A sudden hand movement and the coin is gone.

CONTINUED

23 CONTINUED: 23

KNOCKS
That would have meant that you never had any money if he kept doin' that. You mad maniac.

AMBULANCE MAN
That's what we'd say. - Alan, what ya doin, that was me last penny.. Then he'd clasp his hand like this..

He makes his hand into a fist, crouches in front of Knocks, takes his hand and makes him hold it underneath like a plate.

AMBULANCE MAN
(continuing)
Then he'd ask us to blow on it..

Knocks takes the hint and blows. A pile of coins fall from his hand and drop into Knocks..

AMBULANCE MAN
(continuing)
Then we'd go an buy coffee.

ROMEO
That was all right that was.. Show it again..

AMBULANCE MAN
..Never repeat a trick, rule one of the magic triangle..

KNOCKS
..Circle..

AMBULANCE MAN
..Triangle son.. The circle's for puffs..

24 INT. HOSPITAL. PHYSIOTHERAPY ROOM. DAY 2 24

We see Knocks on a machine in a Physiotherapy room. He is being told how to move and stretch on the machine. He is in quite a lot of pain. We cut to him lying flat on the floor. The nurse is pushing his legs back and turning him over. Knocks lets out a pained expression whenever she pushes too far. The nurse steps back and falls over a ball.

24A INT HOSPIAL CORRIDOR O/S PHYSIO ROOM - DAY 2 24A

We cut outside to the corridoor. Romeo and Sandra are sat drinking coffee. Romeo has some kind of crush on Sandra and is trying to have an adult conversation with her.

ROMEO
Can I get you another coffee.

SANDRA
I'm fine thanks Romeo. He shouldn't be long now.

ROMEO
How's Bill, I've not seen him for ages.

SANDRA
Bill's still Bill.

Sandra pulls a mirror out of her bag and begins to brush her hair.

SANDRA
(continuing)
Look at the bloody state of me.

ROMEO
I think your hairs nice now you don't have it permed it's more natural.

SANDRA
Oh thanks Romeo. That's really sweet of you.

Romeo smiles to himself. He is a leopard with the ladies.

ROMEO
No problem.

24B INT HOSPITAL. HYDROTHERAPY POOL - DAY 2 24B *

(Scene to be written: Romeo, Knocks and Sandra) *

25 INT. ROMEO'S HOUSE. STAIRS. LATE AFTERNOON. DAY 2 25

Romeo is at the top of the stairs. He looks very suspicious. He calls down to his mum.

CONTINUED

25 CONTINUED: 25

ROMEO
Ladine... Mum... Anyone...

There is no reply he rushes back into his bedroom.

26 INT. ROMEO'S HOUSE. BEDROOM. DAY 2 26

He closes the curtains and puts a chair against the wardrobe.

27 EXT. ROMEO'S HOUSE. SIDE PASSAGE/PORCH ROOF. DAY 2 27

We cut to the side of Romeo's house. We see Knocks walking up the side passage. He begins to tentatively climb the ladder leading to the porch roof below Romeo's window. We see him wince as he climbs in slight discomfort.

28 INT/EXT. ROMEO'S HOUSE. BEDROOM. DAY 2 28 *

We cut back inside to Romeo who reaches up to grab the porno magazine they stole earlier. As he is climbing back down there is a massive knock at the window, Bang Bang. Romeo jumps a mile. Falls backwards onto the bed grabbing the curtains for stability. They come tumbling down.

Knocks can now see into the bedroom. Romeo is lying on the bed covered in curtains and pornography. Knocks mouths 'whoops'. Romeo turns round and sees Knocks. He screams at him.

ROMEO
What..

KNOCKS
Erm, are you coming down the park.

ROMEO
Shove it up your arse you stupid loser.

Knocks bursts out laughing.

29 EXT. PARK. EARLY EVENING 2 29

Knocks has presumably left Romeo to sort out the curtains. We see him walk over to the slide in the park and then sit underneath it on a bench. A couple of lads - about 15 years old, are playing football nearby. The ball is miss hit in Knocks' direction.

LAD 1
Kick the ball back..

CONTINUED

29 CONTINUED: 29

KNOCKS
I can't.. I'm awaiting an operation and have to be very careful..

LAD 2
Don't be a knob.

The two approach.

LAD 1
You're 'limpet' aren't you..

KNOCKS
You referring to my walk.. Yes I do have a limp, due to back problems.

LAD 1
Man, you're weird.. What's in ya bag..

KNOCKS
Nothing much..

LAD 1
Let's see then..

KNOCKS
Why don't you get on with your football rather than persist in this stereotypical form of intimidation, which you've obviously picked up from Grange Hill.

LAD 1
What..

KNOCKS
'what's in the bag' is rhetorical..

LAD 2
Do you want a smack in the teeth..

KNOCKS
Why the teeth..

LAD 2
It's a good job your a cripple.

CONTINUED

29 CONTINUED: (2) 29

KNOCKS
I'm not a cripple..

Knocks has tears of rage rolling down his face. Romeo approaches.

ROMEO
What's goin' on.. Are you all right man.

LAD 1
Who are you..

KNOCKS
They're trying to start a fight, 'cause I wouldn't pass them the ball back.

ROMEO
Is that right.

By now Romeo is square on with one of the lads. Without waiting for a response to his question he sends out a fierce punch into the lad's nose.

ROMEO
(continuing)
Come on then.

The lad drops straight to the floor.

LAD 2
A don't fight..

ROMEO
I'll fucking kill ya. You thick bastard.

Romeo pushes the lad back. Knocks moves away. The other lad stands up, blood on face, he starts on Romeo. A two on one fight begins, Knocks backs off.

Romeo is really going for it, but the fact that the lads are older and twice as many sees him loosing. There aren't many clean punches landing. Knocks can't do a thing. Romeo has one of the lads by the throat and will not let go. The other boy is kicking him to try and stop him. Romeo is screaming. There is a lot of aggression for such a young man. A van pulls up at the park and a young bloke gets out, Morell (24). He runs towards the fight.

CONTINUED

29 CONTINUED: (3) 29

MORELL
Oi, Oi, Oi. What's it need two of
you for man. Get off him.

The two older lads back off. He helps Romeo to his feet.

MORELL
(continuing)
You alright Buddy.

Romeo is still very violent. Morell holds onto him.

MORELL
(continuing)
What does it take two of you for
ah.. You pair of fucking tossers..
Go on fuck off.

The lads back off and walk away, scared by Morell. Morell turns to Knocks.

MORELL
(continuing)
Whose team are you on Shirley.

Romeo laughs. He is calming down.

KNOCKS
I can't fight, I'm carrying
injuries.

MORELL
Look at ya mouth man. Ya gonna
need stitches in that fucka.

Knocks inspects the injury like the cut man at a bout.

ROMEO
Oww..Get off

KNOCKS
I think you'll need medical
attention.

MORELL
Is your dad in..

Romeo doesn't answer.

CONTINUED

29 CONTINUED: (4) 29

MORELL
(continuing)
I'll give you a lift up to your house. Can you make it to the van..

ROMEO
Yeah I'm fine.

MORELL
What about you Shirley.. How's the old war wounds.

Romeo laughs again. As they head towards the van.

30 EXT. ROMEO'S HOUSE/STREET. EARLY EVENING 2 30

The van pulls up. Romeo gets out the back. Knocks gets out of the passenger door side. The curtains twitch at Knocks house and his dad comes rushing out the front door looking very stressed.

BILL
What's happened Gavin..

KNOCKS
There's been some trouble down the park.

BILL
Bloody hell Romeo.

MORELL
He's alright mate. It looks worse than it is.

BILL
Gavin what's been bloody happening no-ones hit you have they duck. Is your back alright..

KNOCK
I'm fine.

Ladine comes storming out the house. She looses it slightly.

LADINE
Oh my god.

MORELL
You his mum..

CONTINUED

30 CONTINUED: 30

LADINE
(Quite tearful)
Do I look like a mother..

MORELL
I'll run you down the doctors if you like.

LADINE
I'll just lock the door.

Ladine walks back to the house. We hear something like 'Get Back to what you know' by Embrace.

And we cut back to a birds eye wide shot. We see Ladine and Romeo get back in the van. Knocks and Bill stand and watch the van pull away. We stay on this shot for a few moments.

31 INT. ROMEO'S HOUSE. BEDROOM. EARLY MORNING. DAY 3 31

We cut to the next morning. The music continues. Carol walks into the Bedroom. She had been out till late last night and had not been there for Romeo. It's now about six in the morning. Romeo is asleep lying on his back. We can see the bruising round his face and the stitches in his mouth. Carol sits on the edge of the bed. She feels like shit. A tear rolls down her cheek. She stays there, the music has faded to a close. Pause.

32 EXT. ROMEO'S HOUSE. STREET/FRONT DOOR. MORNING. DAY 332

Morell pulls up in his van. He get's out, jumps the steps and knocks on the front door. He seems smarter than he had previously, as though he's made an effort. Ladine answers the door in her dressing gown. We cut in to her conversation.

MORELL
I just wanted to check he was alright.

LADINE
He's fine. He's the only one who doesn't seem bothered.

MORELL
Tough kid innie.

CONTINUED

32 CONTINUED: 32

LADINE
He's in here if you want to see him..

Pause.

LADINE
(continuing)
Come and have a cup of tea. Me mum'll want to see ya an'all.

Morell answers incredibly quickly. We, and Ladine, get the impression that he fancy's her.

MORELL
Oh yeah lovely gravy.

Morell enters.

33 INT. ROMEO'S HOUSE. LOUNGE. DAY 3 33

We cut to inside a bit later on. Ladine, Carol and Morell are sat having a cup of tea. Romeo is trying to get in on the conversation, so he can get in with Morell.

CAROL
Are you sure you don't want any money for petrol duck.

MORELL
No honest.

ROMEO
I heard one of them lads ended up in hospital Morell.

MORELL
Did he, Why.

ROMEO
Cause I mashed his eye up. It's a good job you stopped me.

Morell laughs. Romeo looks ruffled. His new version of the events is not holding much water.

CAROL
Do you want another cuppa duck.

CONTINUED

MORELL
Ah lovely. I've er not got nothing else on.

LADINE
That's a point, I'd better get ready for work.

MORELL
Where d'ya work Ladine.

LADINE
Jeans Jeans.

MORELL
Next to the tailors Sew and Sew.

ROMEO
That's right opposite the hairdressers Blonde on Blonde.

MORELL
I'll give you a lift down if you like.

LADINE
Lovely. I'll go and get ready.

ROMEO
Can, I get a lift to school please Morell.

Morell pauses. He didn't really want to take Romeo. But can't refuse.

MORELL
Erm... Yeah, I suppose so.

Ladine leaves.

ROMEO
I'll go and fetch Knocks. We've never been in a van before.

Romeo exits. Morell smiles at Carol as though he doesn't mind that his plans have all gone cack.

34 EXT. STREET/OUTSIDE LADINE'S SHOP. DAY 3 34

The van pulls up outside the shop where Ladine works. Knocks and Romeo are sat in the back. Ladine and Morell in the front. The two kids poke their heads through to see out of the front window making it impossible for Morell to ask Ladine out on a date.

LADINE
Thanks alot Morell.

MORELL
Erm, what erm...

LADINE
Yeah..

MORELL
Do you erm... Work here then.

Morell fluffs it.

LADINE
Yeah.. See you then.

She climbs out.

LADINE
(continuing)
See you later girls.

ROMEO
O.K. Bender.

Morell looks really pissed that he couldn't ask her out.

MORELL
Your lip looks a lot better don't it.

ROMEO
Yeah. Why.

MORELL
Nothing. Nothing at all.

KNOCKS
D'ya fancy Ladine.

MORELL
Give us a break..

Knocks bursts out laughing.

CONTINUED

MORELL
(continuing)
Oh forget it.

ROMEO
Don't laugh Knocks.

Trying not to laugh himself.

KNOCKS
He does though.

MORELL
I was going to ask her out you pair of dumb blondes..

ROMEO
You should of said something.

MORELL
I couldn't could I.

ROMEO
She definitely likes ya.

KNOCKS
You can't expect her to go out with you as you are. She works in a clothes shop. I'm just trying to think what she likes... Smart clothes.

MORELL
Suits and that.

ROMEO
Casual. I think you look cool as you are.

MORELL
Nice one Romeo

KNOCKS
She used to go out with the black guy in the shop where she works. He wears all the top gear. Dolce and Gabbana, Woodhouse all that stuff. Loads of sportswear.

34 CONTINUED: (2) 34

MORELL
Fuckin hell man, I've only got Bebe. Romeo you'll have to go and talk to her mate, find out what the crack is

ROMEO
Hows that gonna look, she ain't bloody stupid.

KNOCKS
I'll talk to her. Tell her I fancy some chick and that, need some tips

MORELL
Nice one man. That'll do the trick wun't it Roms.

ROMEO
I dunno, I suppose.

We cut to a wide shot of the three sat in the van. Knocks comes piling out and heads for the shop.

35 INT. LADINE'S SHOP. DAY 3 35

We cut inside the shop.

LADINE
What?

KNOCKS
I've got to ask you something.

LADINE
Your late for school. Can't it wait.

KNOCKS
It's embarrasing.

LADINE
Oh god.

KNOCKS
I fancy this girl at school but i don't know how to impress her.

LADINE
I'm not the girl am I?

CONTINUED

35 CONTINUED: 35

KNOCKS
God no.

LADINE
Fuckin hell thanks.

KNOCKS
I don't mean it like that.

LADINE
All right, what d'ya want to know.

KNOCKS
Just some basic do's and dont's

LADINE
Well you can't really go wrong with jeans and t-shirts, casual stuff you know.

KNOCKS
Levis and that.

LADINE
Yeah that's the kind of thing. everyone's different really. If you play it down with somthing smart and casual, you can't really go to far wrong.

KNOCKS
What about sportwear..

LADINE
Not my thing really. I don't mind tops and that but i can't stand shelleys and all that stuff. I prefer something a bit more subtle.

36 EXT. LADINE'S SHOP/STREET. DAY 3 36

We cut back out to the van. Morell is watching Knocks every move. We see Knocks exit the shop and walk back over to the van. He gets in. Morell wades in.

MORELL
What kind of stuff man, can I do it on the cheap

37 OMITTED 37 *
AND AND
38 38

39 INT. OXFAM. DAY 3 39

Romeo and Knocks are standing outside the changing room in Oxfam. Waiting for Morell. After a short while the curtain opens and out walks Morell in a Ginger shell suit. With a pair of Pink Pony trainers. Romeo and knocks turn away in hysterics. Knocks gives Morell the thumbs up.

40 EXT. LADINE'S SHOP/STREET. DAY 3 40

The three are sat in the van. Ladine is talking in the doorway with her ex-boyfriend Clifford. They are still good friends. Clifford appears quite camp. We cut into the conversation in the van. It must be added that Morell is wearing the Ginger Shelly with an additional lime sports visor.

MORELL
Knocks.

KNOCKS
It's cutting edge Morell stop worrying. Like she said. She likes a bit of spunk.

MORELL
Are you sure there's nothing between them two.

ROMEO
Positive. It was ages ago want it Rom.

KNOCKS
Yer..

MORELL
I wish he'd shove off. I'm forgetting everything now.

CONTINUED

40 CONTINUED: 40

KNOCKS
Just think of the the Fonz.

MORELL
The Fonz wears black and white Man, Not Ginger and Green.

Romeo laughs.

KNOCKS
I'm the only one whose talked to her about men. I know what she likes. Don't I Romeo.

Romeo starts to raise his voice

ROMEO
I don't want any part of it.

The man Ladine is talking too say his goodbyes. Gets on his Honda Melody and drives off. Ladine walks back into the shop. Morell gets out of the van, takes a deep breath and starts to walk over. About half way a car full of youths who know Morell pull up beside him in hysterics. They beep the horn and cheer. He turns round and runs back towards the van He gets back into the van.

KNOCKS
What you doing Morell.. They're just a bunch of idiots.

MORELL
I don't give a toss what anyone thinks. I feel good and that's all that matters. you two follow me to the door and stop people coming in an that.

Morell and the lads get out of the van and head for the shop Morell storms confidently in as Romeo and Knocks stop on the door and look in through the window.

41 INT. LADINE'S SHOP. DAY 3 **41**

We cut inside and Ladine's back is turned. She is putting some stock on the shelves.

MORELL
All right Ladine?

CONTINUED

41 CONTINUED: 41

Ladine turns, sees Morell and laughs.

LADINE
My god, where are you off to.

Pause.

MORELL
I just nipped in to see you.

Pause.

MORELL
(continuing)
Do'ya like erm.

Ladine laughs again. Morell is humiliated. She continues laughing quietly throughout. Morell tries to worm out of it.

MORELL
(continuing)
Yeah I know man yeah, I've got to wear it for work like. A days trial.

LADINE
I didn't think they could be normal clothes.

MORELL
No it ain't man.

Ladine laughs again.

LADINE
There erm...

MORELL
Bright yeah.

It is becoming very uncomfatable. We cut outside to the two boys who are laughing also.

MORELL
(continuing)
I've got a job yer know

LADINE
Oh you've got a job

CONTINUED

41 CONTINUED: (2) 41

MORELL
Er yeah, I'm on trial for the day.

LADINE
What doin?

MORELL
Just cleaning

Morell is saying the first words that enter his head, it is getting worse.

LADINE
Cleaning

MORELL
Cleaning the park... I go round with a brush and that.

He looks down at his clothes.

MORELL
(continuing)
I tried though din't I'

Long pause. Ladine hides her smile. She spots Romeo and Knocks looking in. Morell turns and spots them. Even worse.

MORELL
(continuing)
We'd. I'd better better get back to work. I'll see you later, I'll see you'round.

Morell walks out of the shop devastated. The boys try not to smile. He walks straight past them.

MORELL
(continuing)
Thanks a fucking million.

Morell heads straight for the van. Romeo and Knocks are left standing (laughing) by the shop door.

42 INT. ROMEO'S HOUSE. KITCHEN. DAY 3 42

We cut to Carol making tea in the kitchen. The back door opens. Joseph (Romeo's Dad) is standing in the doorway.

CONTINUED

42 CONTINUED: 42

Carol turns and sees him. She drops a saucepan full of vegetables all over the floor.

43 INT. ROMEO'S HOUSE. LOUNGE. DAY 3 **43**

We are in the living room. Joseph is sat with his bag on the edge of a chair. Carol is still shaky. Smoking a fag. She is on the opposite side of the Room. Joseph is talking very softly and looks quite upset.

CAROL
She chucked you out then, did she.

JOSEPH
No, I left her.

CAROL
I'll bet you did.

JOSEPH
I had to see em Carol

CAROL
You're still a selfish bastard then. Nice you can rely on some things ah.

They sit in silence for a while. The back door goes. Carol holds her hand up to her eyes. Romeo enters and sees his father. He stays cold silent. He just stares at him. Joseph talks to him. Again very softly.

JOSEPH
Alright boy

Romeo doesn't say a word. He continues to stare at him.

JOSEPH
(continuing)
I've cam up to see you for the weekend

Romeo looks at his Mum. She can't look at him.

ROMEO
I'm busy.

He walks straight out of the back door.

44 INT. KNOCKS HOUSE. BEDROOM. LATER. EVENING 3 44

Knocks is in his room. He watches the TV. The door opens and Romeo comes in. The boy is still upset.

KNOCKS
What's wrong..

ROMEO
Dad's turned up..

KNOCKS
Your dad..

ROMEO
Can I stay here tonight..

KNOCKS
Cause ya can..

45 EXT. LADINE'S SHOP/STREET. EVENING 3 45

Morell is sat in the van opposite the clothes shop where Ladine works. He's eating chips out of newspaper. He is listening to the radio, something like 'Got my hand in your head' by Money Mark. Morell sits and watches for a while.

The lights in the shop go off and people exit. Morell beeps his horn and waves to Ladine. She says something to her work mates then comes over to the van.

LADINE
What you do'in here..

MORELL
A thought you might want a lift home..

LADINE
Oh lovely.. How did your job go.

MORELL
I told em to shove it like. Do ya fancy a drink or summut..

LADINE
I don't get paid 'til friday

MORELL
I'll get you a drink an that.

CONTINUED

45 CONTINUED: 45

LADINE
Yer, I suppose..

MORELL
I'll just park up then..

46 INT. KNOCKS HOUSE/BEDROOM. EVENING 3 **46**

We are in Knocks bedroom. Romeo and Knocks are both sat on the bed together. They have the light off. The telly is on. But neither look as though thy are watching. After a short while we hear Sandra calling up the stairs.

SANDRA
Romeo.. Romeo..

47 INT. KNOCKS HOUSE. STAIRS. EVENING 3 **47**

Romeo comes to the top of the stairs.

ROMEO
Yeah.

SANDRA
Your mum's here love. She wants a word with you.

ROMEO
O.K.

Romeo walks down the stairs reservedly.

48 INT. KNOCKS HOUSE. LOUNGE. EVENING 3 **48**

We cut inside to the front room. Carol is sat in Bill's armchair. Romeo stands in the doorway.

CAROL
Sit down duck.

SANDRA
I'll just make a pot of tea.

Sandra exits to kitchen. Romeo sits down on the sofa. It is silent.

CAROL
Ya dad ain't stoppin in the house..

CONTINUED

48 CONTINUED: 48

ROMEO
A've seen him up the garden..

CAROL
He ain't got anywhere to go..

ROMEO
So what's he do'in here then..

CAROL
He wants to see you and Ladine
Romeo..

Outside we hear the muffled beeping of Bills dysfunctional horn.

ROMEO
I ain't interested mum.. He's a
selfish bastard

CAROL
Don't be like that Romeo.. Y'know,
The sooner you see him the sooner
he'll piss off

49 INT. KNOCKS HOUSE. KITCHEN. EVENING 3 49

We cut into the kitchen to see Sandra preparing the tea. Bill comes in through the back door. He goes to walk into the front room - Sandra stops him.

SANDRA
Carol's in there talking to Romeo.

BILL
What you playing at. I want to
watch Jerry Springer, It's the
real alien kid tonight.

SANDRA
Bill.. Joseph came back to see the
kids today.. They've got a few
problems to sort out.

BILL
I don't need this when I get back
from work.. What about tea.

CONTINUED

49 CONTINUED: 49

SANDRA
I've been talkin with Carol all afternoon.

BILL
Can I not even walk through and go and watch it upstairs.

50 INT. KNOCKS HOUSE. LOUNGE. EVENING 3 50

We cut back to Romeo and Carol.

ROMEO
I'm stoppin here tonight.

CAROL
Have you asked sandra..

He nods. The door opens and Bill comes waltzing through. Smiling artificially.

BILL
Dunna mind me.

He exits upstairs very very quickly.

51 INT. KNOCKS HOUSE. BEDROOM. EVENING 3 51

We cut into Knocks' room. Bill comes waltzing in.

BILL
Are you watching this.

KNOCKS
Erm..

52 INT. KNOCKS HOUSE. LOUNGE. EVENING 3 52

We cut back downstairs to Romeo and Carol.

ROMEO
Can I go back upstairs..

CAROL
Go on then. But you got to think about it Romeo.

CONTINUED

52 CONTINUED: 52

Romeo leaves without answering. Sandra comes in with a cup of tea.

SANDRA
There you go.

CAROL
Cheers

SANDRA
How was it..

CAROL
He dun't want to know. Is it still alright for him to stay tonight.

SANDRA
Of course it is.

We hear someone running down the stairs very very quickly. Bill comes into the front room. Carol is in his chair.

BILL
Erm.. Does anyone mind if I just stick the box on.

SANDRA
I do. We're talking.

Bill looks at his watch.

BILL
I'll be in me shed if you need me.

SANDRA
What it in there..

BILL
I can't bloody get channel 5, can I.

Bill walks out

53 INT. PUBLIC HOUSE. NIGHT 3 53

Morell and Ladine are sat in the corner of a very quiet pub, Morell chose this one because he's scared of bumping into any mates. They sip from their glasses and sit in silence for an uncomfortable moment.

CONTINUED

53 CONTINUED: 53

Morell is making a real fool of himself. He's so nervous he can hardly string a sentence together.

MORELL
You like clothes then..

LADINE
I think so.What about you. How did your trial go with that job.

MORELL
It was wank. Oops sorry. Shit. Fuck. Oh Jesus come on man. I can't get a job that suits me really.

Ladine is losing interest fast now. She is begining to realise Morell hasn't got a job.

LADINE
Are you on the dole

Realising this could blow it.

MORELL
No, erm.. Not all the time.

LADINE
Sorry.

She is becoming quite callous. Morell is again Saying the first thing that enters his head. Trying to answer quickly so she doesn't get suspicious. But he taking it to an extreme. The second she stops he flies in.

MORELL
I'm paid for driving me van around you know picking things up...

LADINE
Droppin em off..

MORELL
That's the kind of thing..

They are quiet again.

LADINE
Like a van driver..

CONTINUED

53 CONTINUED: (2) 53

MORELL
Kind of.

LADINE
Ya on the dole then..

Morell gives in to combat the sweating.

MORELL
At the minute like yer.. but there's a few options a'm looking into. A'm thinkin of startin me own business..

LADINE
Doing what..

MORELL
A'm not that far down the line yet..

LADINE
Right..

We stay with them and their next silence for a while, then cut to the next scene.

54 EXT. ROMEO'S HOUSE/STREET. NIGHT 3 54

The van is seen to pull up outside Romeo's house. Romeo and Knocks look out of Knocks' mum's bedroom window. Hoping to read the signs. There are no lights on in the house. They hope not to be seen. We have the impression that everyone else is in bed. We cut into the conversation in the van. Morell still hasn't expressed his feelings towards her. He is about to. Ladine feels awkward. Morells begins.

MORELL
It's been lovely.

LADINE
Yep.. well I'd better get in cause of work.

MORELL
Yer..

LADINE
Ok then..

CONTINUED

54 CONTINUED: 54

MORELL
I er.. I'd like to er..erm.. You want a good night kiss..

LADINE
Oh.. Alright then.

We have the feeling she is going to kiss him to get rid of him. Morell doesn't care either way. She leans over to him and places her hand behind his head. She slowly pulls him towards her, placing his lips to hers for a few seconds and then pulls back, gently stroking his face as her hand moves away.

LADINE
(continuing)
Ok..

Morell nods. We hear cheering from the bedroom window. Ladine gets out of the van and leaves.Highly embbarrased.

We see Morell sigh, very heavily, He sticks his fingers up at Romeo and Knocks, starts his engine then pulls off. He beeps his horn 'da, da, dar der dar dad der dader der der der' it is louder than hell.

55 INT. ROMEO'S HOUSE. KITCHEN. MORNING 4 **55**

Romeo, Carol and Ladine are having breakfast. Ladine is telling Romeo about Morell. Romeo is sticking up for Morell.

LADINE
He's too boring. And he's on the dole. I just felt a bit sorry for him.

ROMEO
You're just being cruel. He really likes you Ladine.

LADINE
You'll understand one day.

ROMEO
That's a bit of a cheap shot. Why did you kiss him..

CONTINUED

55 CONTINUED: 55

LADINE
All right, would you go out with Putty Dowels if she really liked you.

ROMEO
No but she stinks of piss and's got really long gums and tiny teeth.

CAROL
Language.

ROMEO
Sorry.

CAROL
Take a cup of tea up to your dad.

ROMEO
I don't think so. How longs he gonna be at the end of the garden.

CAROL
It's just while he's sorting out a flat.

ROMEO
What so he's moving up here again is he.

CAROL
I can't bloody stop him can I.

LADINE
I'm glad he's come back.

ROMEO
Your unbelievable Ladine. I don't want nothing to do with him, the piece of shit.

CAROL
That's enough.

LADINE
I'll take his tea on my way out.

ROMEO
Got a new pair of trainers coming have you.

CONTINUED

55 CONTINUED: (2) 55

LADINE
I can't believe you just said that.

CAROL
Who does he remind you of Ladine.

56 INT. KNOCKS HOUSE. KITCHEN. MORNING 4 56

Sandra enters the kitchen with a bin bag. She switches the kettle on and sits opposite Knocks at the table. She sighs and stretches out the base of her back.

SANDRA
Oh your back are you love.

KNOCKS
I think so.

Sandra pauses. She turns and takes a letter from the side. Then sits in front of him. Sandra seems slightly pissed off.

KNOCKS
(continuing)
What.

SANDRA
It's come through.

KNOCKS
What.

SANDRA
The date for your operation.

KNOCKS
Right.

SANDRA
Next week.

Knocks falls silent. Sandra puts her arm round him.

KNOCKS
Don't.

He becomes embarrassed by her physical affection. He shrugs her arm off. She snaps at him. We have the feeling she has somthing on her mind.

CONTINUED

56 CONTINUED: 56

SANDRA
Ah, Come on duck. I'd be scared.
So would anyone.

KNOCKS
I'm not scared.

SANDRA
I know duck. Come on. Don't be
funny with me ah.

KNOCKS
It's... just.

Knocks is about to cry. His eyes fill up. Sandra puts her arm back round him. This time he doesn't move away.

Bill calls out to Sandra from outside. Knocks quickly moves away from his mum. He wipes his eyes. Sandra shakes her head and calls to him outside.

SANDRA
What's up..

BILL
We've got raccoons or summut..
Bring us the bleach..

57 EXT. KNOCKS HOUSE. BACK GARDEN. MORNING 4 57

We cut outside to see a shot of Bill bent over looking at a mole hill, prodding it with a stick. A cricket ball travelling at high speed is seen to come from nowhere and hits him on the arse bone. He shouts and bends to help relieve the pain.

58 EXT. ROMEO'S HOUSE. BACK GARDEN. MORNING 4 58

Ladine is seen to leave the house with a cup of tea. She sees Joseph's car parked at the back entrance to the house. She walks up to the car. Inside we see Joseph sleeping. She stands momentarily then taps on the window. Joseph stirs.

LADINE
There's a cup of tea there.

JOSEPH
Thanks darling. You're talking to
me then are you.

CONTINUED

58 CONTINUED: 58

LADINE
Of course I am.

She sits in the car with him.

JOSEPH
I'm sorry I haven't called you.

LADINE
Where've you been dad.

JOSEPH
I went back down London doing a bit of door work.

LADINE
You not in any trouble or anything are you.

JOSEPH
Nah.

LADINE
How long you staying for.

JOSEPH
I don't know yet love.

LADINE
They'll calm down dad. You'll just have to give Romeo a bit of time. I'd better get off dad. Are you OK for money?

JOSEPH
Yeah I'll be alright.

He is obviously skint. She slips him a tenner. He drops his head.

JOSEPH
(continuing)
Thanks darling.

LADINE
I'll see you later dad.

She begins to walk off to work.

59 EXT. PARK. MORNING 4 **59**

Romeo and Knocks walk through the park on the way to school. The two have been walking for a short while. They reach the top end of the park - near to the car park and bowling green, where they see Morell's van parked up. They approach the van and look inside, the windows are steamed up, Morell is asleep and has been since the previous evening after his date.

KNOCKS
He looks dead..

60 EXT. HOT DOG VAN - MORNING 4 **60** *

Morell is eating breakfast. The two lads are sat opposite. Morell looks very tired.

ROMEO
How'd it go with Ladine..

MORELL
It was amazing.. I haven't washed me mouth or anything

ROMEO
Why..

MORELL
'Y'know.. they've got a kiss on em

KNOCKS
Yak..

MORELL
You wouldn't understand would you ya little turd.. You're lucky she said yes knocks. Cause if it had been down to you ya sneaky badger. I'd have been knackered.

KNOCKS
Why you blamin me, what about Romeo, he was laughing an'all

ROMEO
I told him not to knocks, and I made Ladine believe it was a pratical joke.

CONTINUED

60 CONTINUED: 60

MORELL
Yeah that's right. Romeo's a nice person. And your on a YTS for the devil. You toffee teethed maniac.

Romeo laughs.

MORELL
(continuing)
Oh ar.. That Har Karate did the trick. Thanks Romeo.

ROMEO
Thanks for breakfast.

MORELL
No worries man.. You keep me in with your sister and the world's your oyster.

KNOCKS
Can I eat some of that then..

Knocks leans forward to grab some of Morells brekky. Morell slaps his hands with a fork. Knocks jumps and winces as he slightly jars his back.

MORELL
How do'ya do ya back man

KNOCKS
I was born with it I think

MORELL
Born with a bad back..

KNOCKS
Yeah

MORELL
It's not a funny thing a bad back, I had one of them when I was younger. Not as bad as your's though... Once you've done your back, you've done it for life. 'ya know that.

KNOCKS
Well, no not in my case.

CONTINUED

60 CONTINUED: (2) 60

MORELL
Supposed to be true that is you know. It's ruined mens' careers.

KNOCKS
Mine's not like that

MORELL
I had to have mine physiotherapied' by a woman at the hospital. I was at school and I slipped over. I'd go in the room and strip down to my pants and lie on this bed face down. And this nurse came in. And she was foreign.

KNOCKS
I bet she was french an'all want she.

Knocks is rubbing his chin and nodding knowing Morell is talking out of his piecracker.

MORELL
She was just foreign. She want from this country anyway. She used to massage my arse with her thumb. i used to get a real boner. Have you ever had any phsio yourself.

KNOCKS
Little bit yeah.

MORELL
You might get yours felt.

KNOCKS
What.

MORELL
Your ding dong, your dick you maniac.

KNOCKS
Why don't you just get off my back you overgrown pervert.

MORELL
I'm sorry, I didn't know you was gay an that.

CONTINUED

60 CONTINUED: (3) 60

Knocks storms off to the toilet.

ROMEO
Don't Morell. He's got to have an operation next week.

MORELL
Fucking hell, I'm only talking to him. How's that gonna affect it. I don't trust him Romeo. He's a little weasel. I thought you'd ave chosen better company man.

ROMEO
He's just depresssed at the minute.

MORELL
Well it's up to you mate innit.

A waiter comes over. They're the only people in the place, he wants to have a break.

WAITER
You done yet..

MORELL
No..

He goes. Knocks returns from the toilet. He painfully sqeezes back into his seat. Morell looks unconvinced.

ROMEO
What time is it..

KNOCKS
Half Nine.. Shit. We're late for school.

ROMEO
Forget school man.

MORELL
That's the spirit. Let's fuck off for the day. Go to seaside and take in some rays. Let your hair down Shirley you big quasimodo. I need to celebrate.

KNOCKS
What you doing Romeo.

CONTINUED

60 CONTINUED: (4) 60

ROMEO
That, what he just said.

MORELL
Shirley you'll be in hospital soon wun't yar. Give yourself a break, you're like a very old widow.

61 EXT. HOT DOG VAN. MORNING 4 **61** *

We cut to inside the van. Knocks pokes his head through the middle of the seats.

KNOCKS
Where we go'in then.. I'll have to make sure I'm back just after four. So me mum don't click.

MORELL
Lets just drive man. No need to sound like fuckin, er, whatsit..

The van pulls off.

62 INT. MORELL'S VAN. MONTAGE. DAY 4 **62**

A short montage sequence begins. It's almost a jump cut sequence. We are looking down the bonnet at the three of them squeezed in the front, the radio is on. The camera position never changes. We simply jump cut around the different songs on the Radio. First there's a sad song. Everyone is sat looking depressed. Then we cut to a Cajun track, everyone is now freaking out, boogy on down. Next cut. Classical acoustic guitar, Intellectual conversation about the next election. Next cut. Something like 'Who was that Masked Man' by Van Morrison. We cut to wide landscape shots, of the van travelling along the back roads, heading for Chapel St Leonards - a very low grade seaside resort.

63 INT. MORELL'S VAN/HILL OVERLOOKING CHAPEL ST. LEONARDS. DAY 4 **63**

After a while we are looking down a hill and across over to a small seaside town. We see the van driving into town.

64 EXT. SEA FRONT. CHAPEL ST LEONARDS. DAY 4 **64**

We cut onto the sea front. The weather isn't exactly brilliant. They sit on the steps. No-one seems particularly happy or unhappy. The music begins to fade. We cut into their conversation.

MORELL
I used to come here when I was a kid. It's not the same though now. Skegness took a lot of the trade. I hate that don't you. When people pull your memories down and build houses over the top of them.

Knocks leans forward to look at a now philosophical Morell.

KNOCKS
Are you being serious..

Morell throws a shell at Knocks - obviously a one off.

MORELL
Have you seen the rocky films.

ROMEO
Course.

MORELL
There some of the greatest films ever been made. They should be studied really for what they are. there's somthing sentimental in everyone of them to learn from.

ROMEO
Rocky's the greatest.

KNOCKS
Give us a break..

MORELL
You don't understand art do ya shirley..

KNOCKS
No a'm just being honest..

MORELL
Well I don't like it, so shut up ya gay tool.
(more)

CONTINUED

64 CONTINUED: 64

MORELL (cont'd)
I don't want to hear another word out of your big fat cakehole. Your already making me an' Romeo look like a right pair of twats.

Romeo laughs at Knocks instead of standing up for him.

65 EXT. SEA FRONT. CLOSE TO FUNFAIR. DAY 4 **65**

We see our three cowboys walking along the sea front. Knocks has begun to drop behind and seems down, Romeo is fine and happy to communicate with Morell.

They head towards what remains of the fun fair. A few old dodgems. A very old arcade. And a few other bits and pieces.

66 EXT. FUNFAIR. DODGEMS. DAY 4 **66**

Romeo and Morell climb into a dodgem car, remember the two kids have no money. Morell pays for their go and the vehicle sparks into action, both laugh and wail something like the theme to the A -team as the buzz around bashing people. Knocks stands watching them next to the operator. We see them give each other a downward smile - two bored people watching others have fun. He goes into his control box and turns the ride off. We hear Morell booing and then watch them climb out.

67 INT. CAFE. SEA FRONT. AFTERNOON. DAY 4 **67**

The three are in a sea front cafe. They are right by the window. Romeo and Morell are sat together. Knocks sits alone on a table next to them. The tables behind them have been cleared out. Behind them are lots of couples of pensioners dancing. The three continue looking out of the window as the dance takes place. .

68 EXT. ON THE BEACH. DAY 4 **68**

Morell and the two lads have moved down onto the beach. Knocks is looking out to the sea. Morell pulls a fiver out of his pockets.

MORELL
Ice cream boys. Ice cream Knock Knock.

CONTINUED

68 CONTINUED: 68

KNOCKS
Yeah.

ROMEO
I'll have a Cornetto.

MORELL
(To romeo)
Go and fetch em then.

ROMEO
Oh for god's sake, I'll just go everytime.

MORELL
Oh forget about it. I just drove you here din't I.

ROMEO
(To Knocks)
What about this guy..

MORELL
I bought you here Romeo, step to it.

ROMEO
(To morell)
What d'ya want

MORELL
Anything.. As long as it's cold

MORELL
(continuing; To Knocks)
What the hell do'you want.

KNOCKS
I'll have the same as you

ROMEO
I'll remember this

Romeo storms off up the beach. We are left with Morell and Knocks.

MORELL
Having a nice day are you.

CONTINUED

68 CONTINUED: (2) 68

KNOCKS
Yeah

There is a long pause.

MORELL
Just tell me somthing Knock Knock so I can get it straight in my mind. Cause i'm a bit unclear... what was the crack with that situation with Ladine and that with the fucking clothes.

KNOCKS
(Not taking Morell seriously)
Just bad luck mate you want to try flares or sommut next time.

MORELL
What was it all about though.. I couldn't quite grasp it, were you helping me or erm, you know what were you trying to do. What were you trying to get out of it.

KNOCKS
Just trying to help you.

MORELL
Help me..

KNOCKS
Yeah

MORELL
So you wern't joking then you did it for my benefit.

KNOCKS
Yeah

There is a long pause while Morell stares at Knocks. He is begining to unerve Knocks.

KNOCKS
(continuing)
Well no. It might have been a bit of a joke.

CONTINUED

68 CONTINUED: (3) 68

MORELL
Well it worked, Ladine laughed at me.

KNOCKS
Well it's alright now though in't it

MORELL
You made me look a real prick. And you did it on purpose din't ya....

MORELL
(continuing; Long pause. Knocks looks scared)
Why did you try and make me look like a fool Knock Knock. What had I done to you.

Pause.

KNOCKS
Nothing

MORELL
If you want play games, you know if you want to play tricks on people then you've got to recieve a little bit back. Redemption.

Knocks smiles uncomfortably.

MORELL
(continuing)
What you laughin at. I'm not jokin anymore. You can't mess about with peoples feelings like that. You made me look a real fool in front of her, and your gonna pay for it man.

MORELL
(continuing; Another long pause)
I wasn't gonna bring Romeo here today. I was hoping it'd just be me and you. I was gonna blindfold you and take you on a mystery trip like. Into the woods. Do you like the sound of that.

CONTINUED

68 CONTINUED: (4) 68

Knock's is petrified, he daren't raise his head.

MORELL
(continuing)
You watch it Knock Knock, cause I'm gonna get you back. You've made me look a fool and I can't live with that. Are you listening to me.

Morrel puts his hand inside his coat, looks around and pulls out a small knife. He leans over to Knock Knock and puts it to his face. Knocks eyes fill up with tears.

MORELL
(continuing)
I'll tell you somthing for nothing knock knock. You ever fuck me over again an i'll drive this knife right through you. And when i'm done with you then i'll tie your mam and dad to a chair and set fire to em man. Do you understand what you've done to me, are you with me now.

MORELL
(continuing; Knocks nods)
Good boy. Don't you ever play me for a fool again.

Morell moves off and puts the knife back in his coat. We have a moments silence before Romeo comes wandering back over the beach with the ice creams.

MORELL
(continuing)
Ayup.

Romeo sits doown next to Morell. Everyone sits in silence. Knocks is not eating his ice cream.

MORELL
(continuing)
Are you gonna eat that..

ROMEO
I'll have it if you don't want it Knocks..

CONTINUED

68 CONTINUED: (5) 68

KNOCKS
I'm not hungry..

MORELL
Not hungry. Look at the framework on that Romeo. It's like a skeleton. Sometimes I look at you Knocks and I think you look quite pathetic. Would you agree with me.

Romeo laughs.

MORELL
(continuing)
Look at him man he's like a weasel. Sit up straight.

ROMEO
It's not his fault he can't sit up straight.

MORELL
The only thing wrong with his back is that he hasn't got a back bone in it. Look at you. How could anyone rely on you. How could Romeo rely on you for backup, you're an absoloute weasel. Show me some kind of agression. Show me a warrior pose.

ROMEO
Leave it Morell.

MORELL
Show me

He does Judo arms and pulls a face.

MORELL
(continuing)
Come on. Do it..

KNOCKS
I can't.

ROMEO
Just do it Knock Knock, it's only a face.

68 CONTINUED: (6) 68

MORELL
Do it now man.

KNOCKS
No.. Can I not just go..

MORELL
What d'you think..

Silence. There is a real sense that Morell is about to hit Knocks. Morell stands up shaking his head.

MORELL
(continuing)
Come on Romeo.

Morell walks away. After a short pause Romeo follows Morell. Knocks is left sat on the sand. Eventually he gets up on his feet and follows after them.

69 INT. MORELL'S VAN. EVENING 4 **69**

We cut to later that evening. The boys are driving along in the van. Knocks is sat in the back of the van looking out of the window. Romeo is asleep in the front with Morell driving. Time gently passes, we dissolve through the journey. The last moments of peace before the shit hits the van/fan.

70 EXT. KNOCKS HOUSE/STREET. EVENING 4 **70**

The van pulls up. Romeo climbs out and lets Knocks out the back.

KNOCKS
What you do'in now then..

ROMEO
A don't know. See ya later.

He shuts the door and gets back into the front seat. The van pulls away leaving Knocks alone on the curb. His front door opens, Bill appears.

BILL
Gavin.. Gavin..Get in this bloody house now..

He goes inside. The scene fades out.

71 INT. SCHOOL. HALL. (END OF SCHOOL DAY). DAY 5 71

We fade up to the following. The head, Mr. Brown, is standing before the school. We see a few hundred uniformed kids standing with hymn books coming to the end of a song. Everyone eventually sits down.

We see Romeo, he appears isolated from the others - as though he were no longer the child.

MR. BROWN
Right, we'll have all the lads stay behind for an extra ten minutes song practise. If you can't get it right in our time then we'll take up yours, OK. Now, Thursday is non-uniform day. Don't forget your fifty pences. We're going to share the money between the up keeping on Donny the Donkey and Gavin Woolley. Some of you will know Gavin. He's about to have an operation on his bad back.

We see a shot of the lads who had been involved in the fight, and then Romeo.

MR. BROWN
(continuing)
So we think a gift will do him good. Right, any staff messages.

MR. BROWN
(continuing)
Right then, lads stay behind, ladies off you go. Ok Mr. Laws take it away.

The school pianist begins to play the piano as the girls filter out. He's going quite berserk and playing loads of extra bits. Mr. Brown looks over in disgust. The lads go for it a bit more now that the school pianist has souped up the tune.

72 OMITTED 72 *

73 INT. HOSPITAL. OPERATING THEATRE. DAY 5 **73**

Knocks eventually arrives in the theatre.

DOCTOR DOVE
Hello, Gavin isn't it..

KNOCKS
Yes..

DOCTOR DOVE
Hi.. I'm Doctor Dove.. I'll be doing this little operation on your back today ok..

He nods.

DOCTOR DOVE
(continuing)
There's nothing to worry about OK. If you could do me a favour Gavin and start counting as far as you can get for me.

KNOCKS
One..ttt

Knock's eyes flicker as his arm is injected and he sleeps.

74 EXT. SCHOOL. CAR PARK. AFTERNOON. DAY 5 **74**

Romeo walks out of the school. Morell is parked in his van opposite. He approaches and climbs in.

MORELL
What time do'ya call this Sherbet.

ROMEO
The teacher kept me behind asking me why I've been missing an that..

MORELL
Did you tell em what I told you.

ROMEO
Yeah. It worked an'all.

MORELL
It works every time the old adoption number.

75 OMITTED 75 *

76 EXT. LADINE'S SHOP/STREET. DAY 5 76

Morell and Romeo are sat in the van opposite Jean's Jeans. We follow Morells paranoia as he observes Ladine talking to male customers and fellow workers. Romeo is uninterested in Morell's thoughts yet highly interested in his chips. They are listening to the radio. Something like 'T.B Sheets' by van Morrison. Morell sits and watches for a while. Romeo spots his Dad walking along the street, he ducks out of sight. Morell spots him and turns the music up. He pulls off at the highest speed the van will allow. The music continues throughout the next scene.

77 INT. HOSPITAL. WARD. DAY 5 77

We cut to later on. Knocks is asleep in a bed, in a ward now. He's been put in with old men, because there's no room in the children's ward. We see Knocks open his eyes. Sandra is sat beside him, she smiles, squeezes his hand and rubs his cheek. He smiles back.

78 INT. ROMEO'S HOUSE. KITCHEN/BACK DOOR. AFTERNOON. DAY 5 78

Carol and Joseph are sat in the kitchen having a cup of tea. They are trying to talk over what they can do about the kids.

CAROL
I think it might be best if you leave it for a bit Joseph.

JOSEPH
I ain't even 'ad a conversation with Romeo yet Carol.

CAROL *
It's upseting him Joseph. I don't want him feeling he can't come back here cause you're up the garden.

CONTINUED

78 CONTINUED: 78

JOSEPH
All right, well I'll move down the garages. But I ain't leaving yet Carol.

CAROL
That's up to you Joe. *

There's a knock at the door. Carol answers it. Bill is at the door. He sees Joseph and tries to pretend he hasn't.

BILL
Is Romeo ready for the hospital.

CAROL
I'm ever so sorry Bill. He ain't come back yet.

BILL
Oh right.

JOSEPH
Long time no see William.

BILL
Yeah.

Bill doesn't want to speak to Joseph

CAROL
Romeo might be makin his own way up there. I wouldn't hang on for him.

BILL
Alright love.

CAROL
Tell Knocks we're thinking about him.

jOSEPH
Yeah take care Bill..

Bill ignores the goodbyes and wanders off, Carol closes the door.

79 EXT. CORNER SHOP. DAY 5 **79**

We see Morell's van parked outside the local 'Spar' shop. Romeo is sat waiting inside the van. The area seems almost deserted. After a short while Morell exits the shop with a huge bulge in the front of his jacket. He has been stealing food. He gets into the van. We cut to inside. Morell unzips his jacket and pulls out eight packets of crispy pancakes. Romeo looks confused. Morell again pulls off at high speed.

80 INT. MORELL'S FLAT. HALL/LOUNGE. EVENING 5 **80**

Morell and Romeo enter the flat through the front door. We are expecting to see a real shithole with posters and junk everywhere. But it is completly the opposite. It isn't posh or even very nice, it is more like a pensioners flat. There are no signs whatsoever that Morell lives there. We see that one of the downstairs rooms has been made into a bedroom. There is a walking frame, a pair of slippers, and a gas and air cannister by the bed.

Romeo spots this room and stops in his tracks. Morell looks round at him.

MORELL
What?

ROMEO
This ain't your flat.

MORELL
Why?

ROMEO
It looks like some old codgers place.

Morell grabs Romeo by the throat and pushes him up against the wall.

MORELL
Watch your mouth you silly little bastard. It was me dads flat.

He lets go of Romeo's throat and walks off into the front room. Romeo follows him in.

ROMEO
I'm sorry Morell...

CONTINUED

80 CONTINUED: 80

MORELL
I ain't takin you to the hospital now Romeo, you'll have to go on the fuckin bus or summut.

ROMEO
It's too late now anyway.

MORELL
Good.

81 INT. HOSPITAL. WARD. EVENING 5 **81**

Knocks appears more awake, although unable to speak. He still wears his face mask. Sandra is sat with him. Bill enters the ward - as always he appears stressed out. He approaches and starts talking to Sandra

BILL
A couldn't find a space anywhere, It's ridiculous.

SANDRA
Ya dad's here Gavin..

BILL
Ae up son.. He's looking a bit peaky love, is he alright..

SANDRA
Fine a think..

BILL
Does he know we're here..

SANDRA
'Cause he does..

BILL
Ar right, I'd better stay then..

He waves at him.

SANDRA
What does that mean.

CONTINUED

81 CONTINUED: 81

BILL
Well if he didn't know i was here, i could of watched the golden girls.They've got a telly next door.

SANDRA
Jesus Christ.

BILL
Whats wrong with that. It was only if he was unconcious.

82 INT. ROMEO'S HOUSE. LOUNGE/HALLWAY. EVENING 5 82

We cut to shortly after. Romeo and Morell are sat together in the lounge awaiting Ladine. Joseph enters.

JOSEPH
Alright.

He takes a seat.

JOESPH
Have you got anything on tonight Romeo..

ROMEO
A'm go'in to the toilet.

JOSEPH
Alright fine.. Sorry I asked.

Morell turns to Romeo. He wants to wind Joseph up.

MORELL
You can come round mine in the morning if you want Romeo

JOSEPH
You thinkin of adoptin him then..

MORELL
How d'ya mean..

JOSEPH
I ain't hardly seen him, 'cause he's with you all the time..

CONTINUED

82 CONTINUED: 82

ROMEO
It ain't his fault..

JOSEPH
Do me a favour..

ROMEO
Who said you could come in the house anyway.

JOSEPH
What you trying to do to me Romeo. Do you think it's easy trying to talk to you in front of this Joe Palooka.

Ladine enters. The two end their conversation as though the teacher had just walked into class.

JOSEPH
(continuing)
Ae up darlin..

LADINE
Alright dad.. Romeo Sandra came round here this afternoon. Have you been up to the hospital.

ROMEO
Get off my back will ya.

MORELL
Alright Ladine.

He sweats.

LADINE
Romeo said you wanted somethin..

MORELL
Yer.. You want to go outside..

The two head outside. Romeo walks off upstairs leaving Joseph by himself feeling out of place in the front room.

83 INT. HOSPITAL. WARD. DAY 5 **83**

Knocks is now awake. No one has got anything to say. Bill keeps walking up to the door by the corridoor and watching the T.V. we don't see the screen we can just faintly hear some canned laughter Sean and Ronaldo. Sandra is getting very pissed off with him. She is focusing on that rather than Knocks conversation

SANDRA
Bill. Sit down.

KNOCKS
Why didn't you fetch Romeo.

SANDRA
We went round love. There having a bit of a.

Bill bursts out laughing at the programme down the corridoor. Sandra shouts.

SANDRA
(continuing)
Bill, for gods sake. Get in here will ya.

Bill jumps out of his skin. He moans as he walks back to his seat. He goes to sit down when we hear the canned laughter down the corridor really kick in. Bill huffs. He's the look of a broken man.Knocks is fed up of this circus, he is becoming embarrassed. He wants then to leave.

KNOCKS
What time are you staying till, I want to have a plop.

84 EXT. ROMEO'S HOUSE/STREET. EVENING 5 **84**

We rejoin Morell and Ladine who are stood outside, beside the van.

LADINE
It ain't you or nothin ya know that..

MORELL
A don't know what a know and don't know, Y'know.. Me heads a bit lost.. What d'ya mean it ain't me.

Morell is becoming nervous and sweaty.

CONTINUED

84 CONTINUED: 84

LADINE
Well you know my dad and all that...

MORELL
..That's why a want to go for a drink an that, so a can be relaxed and show ya me real side.

Ladine smirks at his streams.

MORELL
(continuing)
Am serious Ladine.. I was thinking about taking you out for a top meal an that. All the lashings. You deserve it dun't you. With the run you've had.

LADINE
It really ain't you.

MORELL
Well come out an I'll help ya, Y'know, forget about it and that man..

LADINE
A don't know..

MORELL
Ar come on Ladine. On me, I'll pick you up drop you home.... Come on It ain't easy asking you know.

LADINE
Alright then.. Next week sometime.

MORELL
Whenever ya want.

Romeo exits from the house. Joseph is stood at the window.

LADINE
I'll see ya later then..

She passes Romeo on her way inside.

MORELL
Nice one mate..

CONTINUED

84 CONTINUED: (2) 84

ROMEO
She say yer..

MORELL
She did..

ROMEO
Brilliant..

MORELL
I'll treat you to a meal for that mate..

ROMEO
Lovely..

They get into the van and drive away. We glimpse Joseph stood at the window.

85 INT. HOSPITAL. CORRIDOR. MORNING. DAY 6 85

Knocks is wheeled along the hospital corridor by Sandra. He's leaving. He has a large plaster cast around his body, making him appear much fatter.

86 OMITTED 86 *

87 INT. BILL'S CAR. STREET. DAY 6 87

We cut to inside the car. Bill is driving slow, so as not to hurt Knocks on any bumps, he is sat in the back bracing himself.

SANDRA
We've sorted out some things with the school. They're gonna be sending some teachers round to help you keep up love..

The horn beeps.

BILL
What a burden, A'm gonna have to get this done.

CONTINUED

87 CONTINUED: 87

SANDRA
You've been sayin that for weeks
Bill..

KNOCKS
Can't we get a new car..

BILL
You gonna buy it are ya..

SANDRA
Bill..

BILL
Well..

We see a shot of a queue of cars stuck behind. The car horn goes off a few times, those behind respond by beeping their horns. We stay with the convoy for a moment then FADE TO BLACK.

88 INT. KNOCKS HOUSE. BEDROOM. MONTAGE. AFTERNOON. DAY 88
7-9

We fade up from black. We go into a montage sequence inside Knocks bedroom, to get an idea of what it's going to be like in his room. As in the van earlier, it will be like a series of jump cuts that show different people sat before Knocks. Once we have the idea, we will watch it all from Knocks' perspective.

Dennis Wardrobe. A very dull and square friend from school.

DENNIS
And then I picked his rubber up
and just threw it..

He laughs.

DENNIS
(continuing)
He thought I was insane.. Y'know
crazy.
Mr. Dudley saw it and said that if
anyone else threw anything we'd
get in trouble. So I was quite
lucky really, Y'know. A could have
got a detention.

CONTINUED

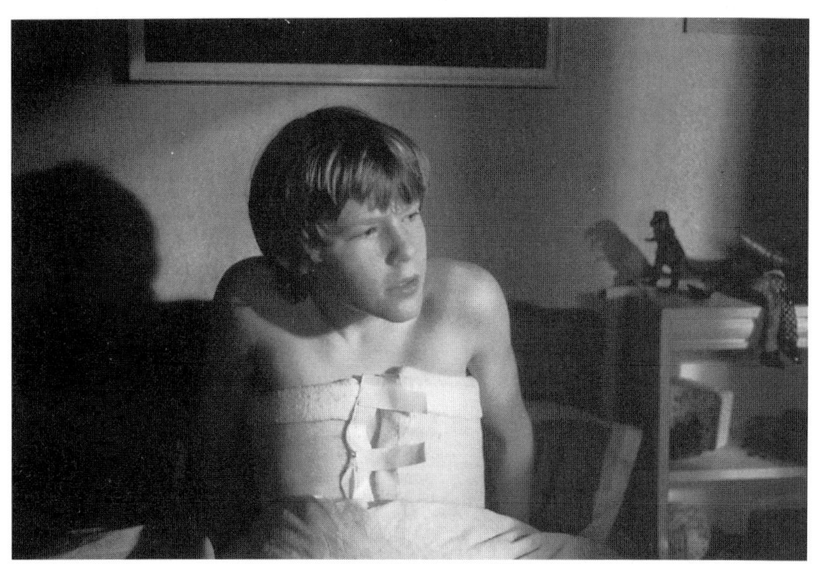

88 CONTINUED: 88

Mr. Bailey, an eight foot biology teacher. He sits opposite with two eggs and a sauce pan. He spins one egg around the other, making car noises. He then extends both arms wide and then bangs the eggs together, smashing them over the pan, some spills over his tweed jacket and un-matching shirt and tie.

MR. BAILEY
And that's called collision.

Mr. Butterbean is the music teacher. He has an acoustic guitar, a big stupid beard and dodgy glasses. He wears a traditional bishop's ceremonial hat. *

MR BUTTERBEAN *
'I am the bishop of our dance.
Come to the Maypole for a
fertility prance. ooooowwaa
ooowwaa.' .. You want to try.

Back to his school friend Dennis.

DENNIS
And Mr. Butterbean said we were going to play a song in front of the school. So me and Mark Rushton did high fives and he told us off. Then he turned away and looked straight back and told us not to pull faces at him when his back was turned. We were really scared, Y'know. And we hadn't actually done a face. That's the thing. We hadn't done anything. *

Mr. Bailey sits with a large tray on his lap. He hums to himself as he sprinkles flour over it, he's acting like the cook on the Muppet show. He opens Knocks' window and attempt to blow the flour out. A gust of wind blows it on him.

MR. BAILEY *
And that's displacement.

Mr. Laws, his English teacher, sits opposite. He's looking through a large pile of papers (stories by Knocks). We watch him slowly fall asleep - his head dropping. An empty can of pop is seen to hit him in the face - Knocks has thrown it. He wakes and looks around the room, then starts to look at the stories again.

89 INT. MORELL'S FLAT. LOUNGE. DAY 9 **89**

Morell and Romeo are stood in the front room. They both have there tops off and are wearing combat trousers. Morell is giving Romeo a lesson in how to knock someone out with one punch. This sequence is all seen in one wide shot. We never cut. Morell is the teacher, Romeo the student.

MORELL
You've got to anticipate, every single thing. You have to be a warrior and anticipate every single thing that might happen.

ROMEO
So it's best to take them by surprise

Morell is in raptures.

MORELL
He's got it. You have ant' ya.

Romeo motions what he has learnt.

ROMEO
If you get them quick, bang there down.

MORELL
Yeah yeah.

ROMEO
If there expecting it.

Romeo winces and tenses his body.

MORELL
That's right

ROMEO
They tense up.

MORELL
He knows.

ROMEO
What do you do when you get hit.

MORELL
Noones ever landed on me. I'm always the first one in.

CONTINUED

89 CONTINUED: 89

ROMEO
Really?

MORELL
I hit first, and ask questions later. That's the philosophy.

ROMEO
Hit first.

MORELL
If your gonna punch someone. Don't stand there going.. Er... You start... No you start.. Er.. Um. if someone starts on me, i just lamp um one. Straight on.. And then i throw it.

MORELL
(continuing; He demonstrates with a straight right hand)
Knockout that is.

ROMEO
Just one punch.

MORELL
That's all you ever need. It's all in the mind see. Somthing goes and then i become unstoppable... totally unstopable.

90 INT. KNOCKS HOUSE. BEDROOM. DAY 10 **90**

The following scene continues from the end of the above montage. Mr. Laws, Knocks' English teacher, is sat on the chair next to Knocks. He has the pile of hand written stories on his lap. He is asleep,head bent forward.

We cut from the previous point of view to see Knocks. He is reading one of the stories to him, unaware that his audience is asleep.

KNOCKS
I thought that friends shared common ground.

He stops.

CONTINUED

90 CONTINUED: 90

KNOCKS
(continuing)
I ended it there.

Mr. Laws rubs his eyes. Obviously very tired and a touch dazed.

MR. LAWS.
Mmm.. That's good..

He yawns.

91 INT. MORELL'S FLAT. LOUNGE. LATER. DAY 10 91

The two are sat in Morell's flat. They are spread across the sofa. They are still sat in their army trousers.

MORELL
How longs your old man gonna stay for.

ROMEO
God knows.

MORELL
He's fuckin things up with me and your sister man.. Can't your mum get rid of him.

ROMEO
She wants us to see him..

MORELL
Don't give into em Romeo. My mum let my old man back every time. Made me life a fuckin misery. I don't want you to end up like me.

ROMEO
Your sound though.

MORELL
It might look like that from the outside Romeo. There's very few people who can penetrate all that. That's why I like you and your sister. You know what I mean mate. We've got a lot in common me and you Rom.
(more)

CONTINUED

91 CONTINUED: 91

MORELL (cont'd)
That's why I'm gonna train you Romeo. Everything i know, i will pass it all on to you.

92 EXT ROMEO'S HOUSE SIDE PASSAGE - DAY 10 92

We see Romeo walk down the side of his house in his school uniform. As he opens his back door we hear Knocks call out from his bedroom: 'Romeo' .Romeo pauses, but ignores it and enters.

93 INT. ROMEO'S HOUSE. KITCHEN/BACK DOOR/LOUNGE AFTERNOON - DAY 10 93

He strolls through to the lounge. Carol is sat in her chair with a fag and cup of tea. Romeo enters without a care in the world having spent another day with Morell rather than go to school.

CAROL
Hiya..

ROMEO
Hello.

CAROL
You want some tea.

ROMEO
No a'm go'in out..

CAROL
Where..

ROMEO
Morells.

CAROL
Can you not stay in please..

ROMEO
He's outside waitin, a said a'd help him move some things in his flat.

CAROL
Your dad's looking for a new flat can't you go and help him.

CONTINUED

93 CONTINUED: 93

ROMEO
You've got to be joking..

CAROL
Well a think ya should Romeo.. And a think ya should go an see Gavin..

ROMEO
A will do.. A'm just lettin him improve a bit

CAROL
He was your best friend a bloody week ago..

ROMEO
I'm gonna go round when i'm good and bloody ready..

CAROL
Don't you fucking swear at me.

He does.

CAROL
(continuing)
You need a smacked arse lad. D'ya hear me. I can smell fags on'ya, I ain't daft. You'd better go round and see him before you go swanning of up there. Sandras been round here three times.

ROMEO
Alright. I was gonna bloody go round anyway. Stick that in your pipe and smoke it.

Carol flies out of the chair at Romeo and smacks him round the face.

CAROL
Don't you ever talk to me like that. You not too big for a bloody good thrashing. Your gonna start doing as your told.

Romeo is shocked. He stands in shaky silence.

CONTINUED

93 CONTINUED: (2) 93

CAROL
(continuing)
Go on, go and see knocks. And then you can go and sort somthing out with your dad. So i can get him to piss off.

94 EXT. ROMEO'S HOUSE/STREET. EVENING 10 **94**

We cut to Morell sat in the van outside . Romeo comes out rubbing his cheek.

MORELL
What's happened man.

ROMEO
Me mums gone spare. She just smacked me really hard round the face.

MORELL
What for?

ROMEO
She's just taking everythimg out on me. I'm going to have to see knocks before we go.I might as well live in a childrens home.

MORELL
Oh come on romeo, what do'ya want to see that plonker for.

ROMEO
I've got to. His mum keeps coming round.

Morell does not want to tell Romeo about the knife incident.

MORELL
I'll come round with ya man if you like. I can pretend we've got to be somewhere by six o'clock.

95 INT. KNOCKS' HOUSE. BEDROOM. EVENING 10 **95**

We cut into Knocks' bedroom. Sandra knocks on the door and enters. Knocks is snoozing.

CONTINUED

95 CONTINUED: 95

SANDRA
Gavin. Romeo and Morell have come to see you.

KNOCKS
Where are they.

SANDRA
He's just waiting downstairs. I said you were sleeping and that i'd just check with you first. Are you O.K.

KNOCKS
I don't want to see anybody mum.

Knocks falls silent.

SANDRA
A... A... Come on duckie. Yuo don't have to see people if you don't want too

She puts her arm round him.

SANDRA
(continuing)
It's O.K. Love. Don't worry about it. I'll tell them your not up to it.

96 EXT. ROMEO'S HOUSE/STREET - NIGHT 10 96

We hear a song like 'Gypsy' by Van Morrison. We see a shot of our semi detached house at nightfall. The curtains are closed in both houses but the lights are on in both front rooms.

96A INT KNOCKS HOUSE. BEDROOM - MORNING 11 96A

We cut to the next day. Where we see Knocks who is sticking a poker down his plaster cast to scratch his chest.

96B EXT LOCK UP GARAGES - DAY 11 96B

Then we begin to intercut. First we see Morell and Romeo parked up in some garages. This wide shot will be highly composed, with the camouflage van set in between the multi-coloured doors of the garages.

96C INT KNOCKS' HOUSE. BEDROOM - DAY 11 96C

Then we cut back to Knocks who has drawn on a coal moustache and is using his dinner tray to try out some card tricks. He is trying out some patter with it, calling himself 'Italian Mick' and speaking with a heavy accent.

96D EXT. A ANOTHER LOCK UP GARAGES - DAY 11 96D

We cut back to Romeo and Morell at a different set of garages This time they are kicking a football against one of the garage doors. We hear the crashing metal everytime Morell hoofs it.

96E INT KNOCKS HOUSE. BEDROOM - DAY 11 96E

We cut back to Knocks who has gone for a beard now. His name has changed to 'Eddie Fantastic' and his accent is now that of a quick talking New Yorker.

96F EXT. A ANOTHER LOCK UP GARAGES - DAY 11 96F

We cut back to Morell and Romeo. Romeo is stood with his eyes shut whilst Morell moves around him silently then screams. Romeos responses are gauged by Morell. They talk intellectually in between each one, discussing how Romeo can speed up his reactions.

96G EXT ROMEO'S/KNOCKS' HOUSE (STREET) - DUSK 11 96G *

We cut outside Knocks' house to see Mr. Laws exit from Knocks'. He unlocks his bike from the post outside the house and rides off. Morell pulls up in the van and beeps his horn.

Romeo gets out of the van, Ladine exits the house passing Romeo on the steps and gets into the van. They drive off. Bill arrives in his car, he pulls up, his horn beeps. We cut to the next scene. The music begins to fade.

97 INT. ROMEO'S HOUSE. LOUNGE/FRONT DOOR. EVENING 11 97

Romeo is sat in the lounge with Carol. There is a knock at the door. Romeo looks at Carol. Carol stares at Romeo, he gets up and answers the door. Joseph is stood in the door.

JOSEPH
You free I take it then Romeo..

CONTINUED

97 CONTINUED: 97

ROMEO
What..

JOSEPH
Morell just road past me.

ROMEO
He's taken Ladine out.

JOSEPH
It's alright, I've come round to see you.

ROMEO
Why..

JOSEPH
'Why'..

ROMEO
Why the sudden interest, Y'know what a mean..

JOSEPH
I wanna try and facking sort things out a bit..

ROMEO
I'm not interested Dad.

JOSEPH
Get ya coat. Go on just come for a drink.

98 AND 99 OMITTED 98 AND 99 *

100 INT. KNOCKS HOUSE. BEDROOM. EVENING 11 100

Knocks is watching the cricket highlights, the TV is low, there is a relaxed feeling in the room for the first time.

CONTINUED

100 CONTINUED: 100

He sits with a ball of elastic bands, he has a pile of loose ones which he is adding to the ball, occasionally glancing at the cricket. We see him do this for a while prior to Sandra entering. She's a little tipsy from a night out playing darts, making Knocks uneasy.

SANDRA
Alright love..

KNOCKS
Yer am fine..

SANDRA
Ya been for a poo tonight..

KNOCKS
Not yet..

SANDRA
I told him to bloody take yer..

KNOCKS
I didn't need one.

SANDRA
Do ya want one now..

KNOCKS
No I don't bloody want one.
Flippin heck

SANDRA
Alright sorry.. Bloody hell Gavin
give me a break ah love.

KNOCKS
It's late..

Silence. Sandra goes to leave.

SANDRA
O.K. Goodnight. Love you.

KNOCKS
Yeah...like you.

We hear and then see the end credits of the cricket. Knocks uses his walking stick to reach the off button, he misses and drops the stick. He returns to putting bands onto his ball.

101 INT. KIDS PUB. EVENING 11 **101**

We see Joseph and Romeo sat alone in the kids room at the Vaults. The room is obviously designed for toddlers. Tiny chairs and cartoon characters on the wall. Joseph and Romeo are hunched up on two tiny plastic green chairs in total silence. Joseph looks around the room. Romeo reaches for his coke drinks it all down in one go then sits back and leans on the teenage mutant hero turtle table. At this silent point we see Three Attractive Young Girls walk past the window outside the kids' room where the two are sat. They look in at Romeo and his dad cramped up round the turtle table and burst out laughing. Romeo is humiliated. He puts his hand over his eyes.

102 INT. KNOCKS HOUSE. BEDROOM. NIGHT 11 **102**

We see the image of the BBC globe spinning. Knocks has just placed his last elastic band onto the ball and throws it against the wall. He catches it.

KNOCKS
And he's gone.. Caught by Woolley
at silly mid off..

TV ANNOUNCER
And now on one, our late night
film. The erotic thriller Mandy
Muzzongers Is The Dirty Filthy
Detective.

Knocks turns his head to the TV. We see the film has started. The opening credits pass.

The scene is now awash with naked bodies. Knocks stares at the images. The first time that he has seen nakedness and motion together. Without seeing anything, we understand that he has an erection. He reaches to feel the event, and whispers 'oh shit'. We see a full view of Knocks in his room. The TV is now pumping out hard core images to this once innocent mind. His knees are raised, hiding the mini sausage protrusion that has come up for air.

KNOCKS
Mum.. Muum.. Muuummm..

103 EXT. MORELL'S FLAT. COURTYARD. NIGHT 11 **103**

The van arrives at the courtyard leading to Morell's block of flats. He gets out of the car. Ladine follows. They walk to the steps.

104 INT. MORELL'S FLAT. LOUNGE. NIGHT 11 **104**

We cut to inside. Morell pushes the junk off the sofa removes the used cups from the coffee table. He exits to get Ladine a drink. We stay with her, she sits and looks around. She sees Romeo's school bag. She shouts through to him.

LADINE
Do you live with your grandad.

MORELL
No.

LADINE
Right.

Ladine looks around the flat looking a bit confused. She spots Romeo's bag.

LADINE
(continuing)
What's Romeo's bag do'in' here..

MORELL
Ah..

She places it by her leg, so she can take it with her.

LADINE
Already furnished then was it..

MORELL
Yeah.

He sits beside her. She's fine and comfortable, he's awkward with the whole thing. Nothing is said for a moment.

MORELL
(continuing)
Shell I put the TV on.

LADINE
Yer why not..

He does. It's an old black and white. You have to turn a dial to tune into a channel. He finds the setting. A none porn bit to 'The Bitch'. He sits back.

MORELL
You watch much TV.

CONTINUED

104 CONTINUED: 104

LADINE
Not really.. A spend a lot of time in me room at home.

MORELL
I spend most of my time in my van..

They go quiet and watch the screen. A rude bit comes up, they don't speak, both stare at it. Morell's head has gone now. He's incredible awkward. He's sitting watching sex scenes with someone he's being thinking of having sex with all night, he doesn't know where to put himself, other than to get out. That's what he does. He exits to his room.

MORELL
(continuing)
Won't be a minute..

Ladine remains sat watching the rude antics of those on screen. She has a look on her face as if she's thinking 'how on earth do they manage to do that'.

105 EXT. ROMEO'S HOUSE. BACK GARDEN. NIGHT 11 105

Romeo and Joseph pull up in the car at the back of the garden where Joseph sleeps. The car engine turns off.

We cut into their conversation. Joseph is trying to apologise for the nights events.

JOSEPH
I'm really sorry about tonight son. I dun't want it to start off like this.

ROMEO
Start. I don't need you round me Why don't you just piss off.

Romeo gets out the car and walks off down the path. Joseph doesn't bother trying to stop him. We stay with Joseph for a while sat in silence. We hear the back door close off camera, as Romeo enters the house.

106 INT. ROMEO'S HOUSE. KITCHEN/LOUNGE. NIGHT 11 106

Romeo enters. We pass into the kitchen. Carol is also watching the erotic thriller.

CONTINUED

106 CONTINUED: 106

ROMEO
A'm go'in to bed.. What's this..

CAROL
Never you mind.. You had a nice time..

ROMEO
Fine.

CAROL
How'd it go..

ROMEO
Fine..

Romeo goes off to bed. Carol shrugs and returns her attention to the film.

CAROL
Oh my Gawd..

107 INT. MORELL'S FLAT. LOUNGE. NIGHT 11 107

Ladine is still watching the film. We hear Morell call her. She asks him what he wants. He persists. She gets up and goes to the stairs.

108 INT. MORELL'S FLAT. STAIRS/LANDING. NIGHT 11 108

Morell asks her to come up again - to show her something. She climbs the stair and picks a door, the bathroom, she closes it and tries the next.

109 INT. MORELL'S FLAT. BEDROOM. NIGHT 11 109

We cut to inside as the door swings open. Morell is on the bed, naked apart from a short silky looking night-gown. He goes to untie the belt around his waist.

MORELL
You comin in..

The belt falls to either side. We see a view from behind Ladine, her head hides the rude bits.

LADINE
Oh my God.. Oh my god..

CONTINUED

109 CONTINUED: 109

She's shaking her head, half in shock, half in hysterics.

LADINE
(continuing)
Bye..

110 INT. MORELL'S FLAT. STAIRS/LANDING. NIGHT 11 110

Ladine closes the door and goes down the stairs. Morell reopens it, pulling the gown back together as he too heads for the stairs. Ladine grabs her coat and Romeo's school bag.*

LADINE *
Don't say anything Morell, You'll *
make it worse.. *

MORELL *
A thought.. *

LADINE *
A really don't want to know the *
thought process.. A really don't.. *

MORELL *
Ladine.. Don't go.. A can get *
changed Ladine.. A'm sorry.. Come *
on.. *

Ladine moves past him. She's strong enough not to be scared *
or intimidated by any of this, she passes him and leaves. *
Morell turns and follows her to the door. *

111 OMITTED 111 *

112 EXT. KNOCKS HOUSE/STREET. MORNING 12 112

We see Mr Laws pull up on a pushbike outside Knocks' house. Bill is in the garden tipping bleach on various unspecified lumps. Steven watches with interest. After a short while Bill looks up too see Steven.

BILL
They bloody back again.

CONTINUED

112 CONTINUED: 112

STEVE
Right.

BILL
This is industrial.

Bill lifts the bottle of bleach up to Steve. Steve pretends that he knows what he's on about.

STEVE
Yeah. Right. Good. I'll see you then.

Bill is already back wandering round the garden, Steven walks up the path to Knocks' house.

113 INT. KNOCKS HOUSE. BEDROOM. MORNING 12 113

We cut upstairs to Steven and Knocks in the bedroom. Knocks is reading out another one of his stories.

KNOCKS
The boy got up when his alarm went off. He put on his biggest overcoat because he didn't know the secret of getting rid of a big dingaling. A lot of people walk around in big coats because they don't know the secret. His mum thought that people watch too many Carry On films..

He stops. Mr. Laws has started to snore. He's looking confused, he's not sure what to do. He taps him a few times. Nothing. He puts his book down and pulls his magic tray towards him, he begins practising again.

KNOCKS
(continuing)
When I was young I was thrown out of my home by my evil stepfather. I had no way of making money, so I had no food.

As he speaks he takes three metalic cups and moves them around on the box. He then takes one dried pea and places it on top of the cup. He then places the other two cups on top of this one then taps the top. He lifts the cup to show that the pea has travelled through. We see him mess the trick up slightly but he is getting better and more confident.

CONTINUED

113 CONTINUED: 113

KNOCKS
(continuing)
So I had to learn to make my own food.

114 EXT. PARK. MORNING 12 **114**

Morell is asleep in his van in the park.The bottle of fizzy wine on his lap. The windows are steamed up. Romeo approaches it, dressed in his uniform. He opens the passenger door and gets in. We cut to inside. Morell slowly wakes. He's hung over.

MORELL
Arr, urrgg.. Oh man.

He puts his face in his hands and remains silent.

ROMEO
Good night was it..

MORELL
Mmm.. urr, a'm gonna be sick..

He opens the door, leans out and vomits. Romeo laughs at him.

115 INT. KNOCKS HOUSE. BEDROOM. MORNING 12 **115**

Mr. Laws is sat in the bedroom. As always, he is tired. They sit in silence for a while.

KNOCKS
Are you being paid any extra for these sessions

MR. LAWS
How d'ya mean..

KNOCKS
You just fall asleep.

MR. LAWS
A don't..

KNOCKS
Ya do every,time. I get half way down the page and you're gone..

CONTINUED

115 CONTINUED: 115

MR. LAWS
A'm sorry Gavin.. I can't really talk to you about it. But it's nothing to do with you..

KNOCKS
And why do'ya stink.

MR, LAWS
I don't stink do I.

KNOCKS
Not of poo or anything, it's kind of Biscuity..

He smiles, Knocks smiles back and raises his eyebrows.

MR LAWS
A'm in the middle of a divorce.

KNOCKS
Which is bad...

MR. LAWS
Yer..

116 EXT. LADINE'S SHOP/STREET. DAY 12 116

The two are sat watching the shop. Ladine can be seen inside with Clifford. Both are in stitches - we assume she's telling him about Morell. In the van things are tense. Morell has a real grimace on his face, he knows what they're talking about. We see a shot of Ladine doing an impression of Morell's position on the bed. They're crying with laughter.

ROMEO
There probably talking about somethin else.

MORELL
Like what..

Romeo has no answer, we all know what she is saying

MORELL
(continuing)
I might as well fucking kill myself.
(more)

CONTINUED

116 CONTINUED: 116

MORELL (cont'd)
It'll be all round town with that fucking Gaylord on the case wun't it. I'm gonna be a laughing stock. Your gonna have to help me Romeo.

ROMEO
What can i do. You go in, at least she's laughing.

MORELL
What kind of a silly bastard are ya. This is important Romeo. If you ain't gonna help me you may as well just shove off... Go on...

Romeo is being blackmailed.

ROMEO
What d'ya want me to do.

MORELL
Tell her about the real me. The tender side. Tell her about me being fostered an all that.

ROMEO
Ae..

MORELL
Just fuckin step to it and make it sad.

Romeo gets out and walks to the shop. Morell puts his hands together in some kind of religious praying shape, slightly wrong of course.

117 INT. LADINE'S SHOP. DAY 12 **117**

We cut inside to Romeo standing talking to Ladine. Clifford is shaking his head.

LADINE
You've got to be joking Romeo, d'ya know what he did.

ROMEO
His mum dropped him down the stairs when he was a baby.

CONTINUED

117 CONTINUED: 117

LADINE
Give it break, He's a pervert, you want to fucking watch yourself. What the fuck is with his flat.

ROMEO
He's just confused. His Nan used to sleep with him.

118 EXT. LADINE'S SHOP/STREET. DAY 12 **118**

We cut back into the van. Romeo jumps back in trying to look hopeful.

MORELL
What happened man?

ROMEO
Er.. She's erm, ya know she needs abit of time. She never promised or anything.

Romeo is lying. Morell doesn't want to notice.

MORELL
Romeo your a diamond. Your like a brother to me.You won't let me down will ya. You know what Ladine means to me.

Romeo smiles unconvincingly.He is digging a hole for himself.

119 INT. KNOCKS HOUSE. BEDROOM. MONTAGE. DAY 12 **119**

We begin with Mr Laws sat on a chair next to Knocks. He is rambling on about the divorce. We see Knocks lying on his bed. Looking up to the ceiling.

119A INT KNOCKS HOUSE. BEDROOM - MONTAGE - DAY 12 **119A**

We cut to Bill sitting in front of Knocks looking at his watch, hoping he's been there long enough and then...

119B INT KNOCKS HOUSE. BEDROOM - MONTAGE - DAY 12 **119B**

We cut to the Physiotherapist who is turning Knocks over in bed and stretching his legs.

119C INT KNOCKS HOUSE. BEDROOM - MONTAGE - DAY 12 119C

Finally we cut into Sandra who brings Knocks his tea. She tidies around his room as he writes into his book. We cut to a short while later. Sandra has stayed in the room. Now Knocks is asleep. She is sat on a chair next to him reading from his book.The sunlight pushes the window frames reflection over the bed. The window moves gently across the bed onto the wall, as the sun moves outside. We only hear the following poem. Knocks lies in silence.

KNOCKS (V.O.)
The mustard layered lollipop lady. Battered and beaten though baked in beauty is idolised by child and driver alike.Cycling to provide. Her worn shoes slip on the wet peddles of the swelling tires, condemning the illuminated school queen to the illusion of the bobby on his bike, or Bunty riding down the lane. Paradise is too far, like a three minute mile on square wheeled roller blades. I've chased it's warm glow for some time.

A slight pause before the scene fades out.

119D EXT. ROMEO'S HOUSE. FRONT GARDEN. DAY 119D *

We see Romeo leave the house in his school uniform. He is *
setting off to school. *

120 INT. MORELL'S FLAT. LOUNGE. MORNING 13 120

We fade up to the following. Romeo has fallen into the role of a kitchen tied spouse. We see him preparing breakfast and making the coffee, whilst Morell lounges on the sofa. He sips his drink, it tastes shit, so he gives it back to Romeo who goes off to make another for him. Morell calls to Romeo in the kitchen.

MORELL
And Romeo run down to the town an'all man and get some Crispy pancakes man. We've only got one box left.

121 EXT. KNOCKS HOUSE. BACK DOOR. DAY 13 121

We see Dennis Wardrobe arrive and Knock on the back door. Sandra answers and we cut upstairs.

122 INT. KNOCKS HOUSE. BEDROOM. DAY 13 122

Knocks hates Dennis pretty much. Dennis enters. Knocks is having a wee wee under his bedcovers into a bottle.

DENNIS
Don't mind me..

KNOCKS
Have you ever heard of knocking Dennis..

DENNIS
I'll face the telly.

KNOCKS
Go outside a minute, I'm trying to have a piss. I'll call you when I'm finished.

Dennis walks outside the door. We hear Mr Laws come round the back on his bike. We cut to a shot of Knocks, shifting himself carefully around on his bed so he can get a view out of the window. Sandra comes down the path from putting out her washing to greet him. We hear her ask with concern if he's alright. Knocks twists to see if he can see what's going on. Dennis walks back in to the room.

DENNIS
You done.

Knocks can't listen because of this interruption.

KNOCKS
Look just piss off Dennis you friggin arsebag.

123 EXT. KNOCKS HOUSE. BACK GARDEN. DAY 13 123

We cut back in the garden. Sandra is sat on the lawn talking to Mr Laws who looks very depressed.

SANDRA
Do'ya want a cup of tea Steve...

MR. LAWS
Oh you don't want to be bogged down with my life..

Steven is fishing for lilies

CONTINUED

123 CONTINUED: 123

SANDRA
I don't mind at all. It's good to talk to someone not involved sometimes.

At that point Dennis comes storming out of the house. Sandra calls out to him.

SANDRA
(continuing)
Dennis what's wrong..

DENNIS
Ask Schizo face.

Dennis storms off. Sandra laughs under her breath. She turns back to Steven. He isn't laughing she tries to look concerned.

We see Knocks sat looking out of the window down onto Sandra and Steve who are talking. Bill walks round the side of the house, returning from work. Knocks watches as Bill makes a turd of himself. Bill sees Sandra in her shorts and bikini top.

BILL
What's go'in on here then..

SANDRA
Stevens just had some bad news..

BILL
Did he buy you those clothes as well did he.

SANDRA
Oh my god, don't do this Bill..

He stands for a moment, his suspicious mind playing tricks.

BILL
Well look at ya..Go and put some real clothes on.

MR. LAWS
I'd better go up and see Gavin

SANDRA
Take no notice Steve.

CONTINUED

123 CONTINUED: (2) 123

BILL
That's bloody right.You stay there
Steve I'll go and bloody....

Bill storms off into the house. Looking back twice to see if anyone is interested.

124 INT. MORELL'S FLAT. KITCHEN/LOUNGE. AFTERNOON. DAY 1124

Romeo enters with some stolen food up his jacket. He walks through the kitchen into the lounge undoing his coat to take the stolen goods out. We think he's alone for a moment, then Morell jumps out from behind the door wearing stocking over his face.

MORELL
Argh..

ROMEO
Argh..

Morell starts to laugh..

ROMEO
(continuing)
What ya do'in ya idiot.

MORELL
Don't be like that ya mardy arse..

ROMEO
What ya do'in jumpin out on me
then ya friggin cock smoker.. It's
not funny.

MORELL
It was a joke man..

ROMEO
..Not funny.

MORELL
Have you ever done the business.

ROMEO
What d'ya mean,What's the 'Busines'

MORELL
The business man. With a chick.

CONTINUED

124 CONTINUED: 124

ROMEO
Cause I haven't..

MORELL
Go in there man. It's been waiting all afternoon.

Romeo huffs and opens the front room door. There is a women in her twenties sat watching the telly. Romeo closes the door and looks at Morell.

ROMEO
Who's that.

MORELL
She'll do the bizz. You onna scared are you.

ROMEO
I don't even know her do i.

MORELL
It's perfect that is. It dun't matter if you're shit.

ROMEO
I'm not doing anything with her.

MORELL
What are you a man or a mouse. Get in there man she thinks your eighteen.

ROMEO
Why are you being so nasty to her.

MORELL
You don't understand anything do ya. Ya not a man at all are ya. when i was your age, i'd have been in there like a maniac.You have'nt taken any notice have you.

ROMEO
I don't want to.You bloody idiot

MORELL
Well i won't try and help you again. Make me look a right prick. Your as bad as shirley.

CONTINUED

124 CONTINUED: (2) 124

ROMEO
Oh piss off Morell.

Morell grabs Romeo.

MORELL
Your lucky I'm with your sister you cheeky little muppet. Watch your mouth and show a bit of respect.

Romeo is really shaky. He has tears in his eyes.

ROMEO
Yeah right. Get your hands off me.

Morell lets go of him.

MORELL
Don't cry man, whats wrong with you.

ROMEO
I don't believe you Morell.

Romeo walks off. Morell calls after him.

MORELL
Don't you say anything to Ladine about this Romeo. I thought you might of wanted the ride man. Obviously not. *

125 OMITTED 125 *

126 INT KNOCKS HOUSE. BEDROOM - DAY 13 126

MR. LAWS
Alright then..

KNOCKS
Good thanks.. You.

CONTINUED

RYING SCOTSMA
Fayre
SCOTLAND
LISTS

126 CONTINUED: 126

MR. LAWS
Yer not bad.. Well.. not to good really. I got a letter from her solicitor this morning... She's trying to ruin me Gavin. Can you believe that.

KNOCKS
Erm..

MR. LAWS
Bloody women. She'll stop at nothing. I've got a bloody ulcer through all this. I can't eat any kind of spicy food.

Knocks is bored already, he sits and looks on as Mr laws continues on another trip down memory lane.

MR. LAWS
(continuing)
It's been like a haven coming here you know. Well with her teaching at the same school an everything. I think I'd have gone mad if it wasn't for this. I don't have to pretend when I'm in here.

Knocks looks up at him and tries to smile.

127 INT. KNOCKS HOUSE. BEDROOM. EVENING. 13 127

Knocks is in his bed, he's writting in his book. An argument between his mum and dad begins off camera. He puts his book down to listen in.

His bedroom door is opened, he is seen to be straining to get a better position to hear them. We can hear a row going on downstairs. Bill is accusing Sandra of having an affair. Sandra is trying to stay calm and laugh it off.

128 INT. KNOCKS HOUSE. KITCHEN. EVENING 13 128

We cut downstairs to them arguing.

SANDRA
Don't be so bloody daft. You never bloody bother any other time, so why start now.

CONTINUED

128 CONTINUED: 128

BILL
He's a bloody eccentric in't e.
He'll be bloody wearing hippy juice an all that Jazz.
He's pretending to be a weirdo, so you'll think he's different and so you'll go off me. well I'm not having it Sandra do you hear me.
He's not coming round here again.

Sandra laughs at first then explodes.

SANDRA
Who the fucking hell do you think you are. You've got no right to tell me anything about what I can do with my life. I put up with absolutely every design fault going in this bloody house. My son's going through bloody murder and you go out, work in your silly bloody shed, well you might as well just pack your stuff and piss off Bill. 'Cause if you don't I will. I can't stand another minute with you, you selfish... Shitbag.

BILL
You want to go..

SANDRA
Don't push it bill

BILL
A feel like ya just messin' with me.. Ya tryin' to get me to say go aren't ya, so ya don't feel like your the one endin it..

SANDRA
I'm not the selfish one Bill.
Gavins not been himself at all and all you can think about is your silly fuckin' self.

BILL
Don't bring the kid into it again Sandra.. Anyone'd be depressed after an operation.

CONTINUED

128 CONTINUED: (2) 128

SANDRA
You make me sick you ignorant bastard. There's no point carrying on. If it wasn't for Gavin I'd've left you ten years ago Bill.

BILL
What was that.

We cut upstairs as the silence hits the floor. We see Knocks sat in silence. We stay in Knock's room as we hear Bill.

BILL
(continuing)
Why don't you just piss off with Dennis bloody Hopper then, I'll not stand in your way anymore

Bill storms out of the house.

129 EXT. ROMEO. MONTAGE SEQUENCE - DAY 13/NIGHT 13 129

We hear music like '10th Story love song' by the Stone Roses. We begin a montage sequence charting Romeos afternoon. As he wanders the bare landscapes of the almost empty town and fields alone. This is really the first time in the film that we really see Romeo as a child. The music runs throughout this sequence allowing us to breathe in Romeo's company. As the music fades we cut to the evening with Romeo walking back up the side passage if his home. He doesn't enter though. He stands on the back and gathers some pebbles from the garden. After a short while he begins tossing them up at Knocks' window next door trying to wake him. He calls quietly after hitting the window.

ROMEO
Knocks....

Another successful stone.

ROMEO
(continuing)
Knocks...

We hear Bill from inside his his shed call out in a state of massive depression

CONTINUED

129 CONTINUED: 129

BILL
Give over Romeo will ya. It's no good round here anymore. Just stay away, it's all gone bad.

130 INT. KNOCKS HOUSE. BEDROOM. NIGHT 13 130

We cut inside to Knocks' bedroom. Rather than being asleep he is sat wide awake in his room working on his new magic character 'Clive Merlinium'. We stay inside as the next stone hits the window and we hear Romeo call out once more. We hear Bill once more say 'Keep away'. Knocks quite coldly ignores them both. After a while it falls silent. Knocks pulls himself over towards the curtains. He looks out onto Romeo's back garden. He has left. The light is on in Bill's shed. Knocks turns the telly on and sits back in bed. We cut away to a wide shot behind Knocks' and Romeo's house. It continues on from the previous scene. We can see Knocks' bedroom light flick on. And we hear the first line from the short story.

130A INT ROMEO'S HOUSE LOUNGE. NIGHT 13 130A *

(Scene to be written: Carol and Sandra) *

131 EXT. ROMEO'S HOUSE/STREET. NIGHT 13 131

As the first line is read, we see a shot of Morell parked up in an empty car park in town. He puts his radio on, then opens a can of special brew. After a moment we see a shot of Ladine and her new date, Darren, walk past. Morell's face falls apart in front of our eyes.

KNOCKS (V.O.)
Blow up a tall building if you think it'll make a difference.

132 INT/ EXT. BILL'S SHED. NIGHT 13 132

Bill is sat in his shed. He is seen to be physically taking his agression out on objects in the shed. He fiddles with his aerial for a better reception, to no avail. We cut outside, a few bangs etc. The aerial is thrown out the window.

KNOCKS (V.O.)
Fill up a barrel of dynamite and blow it sky high.

133 EXT. GARAGES. NIGHT 13 133

We see Joseph sitting in his van. He sits in silence for a few seconds then lights a cigarette, lies back in his seat and puts his feet out of the window.

134 INT. ROMEO'S HOUSE. LOUNGE - NIGHT 13 134

Then we cut into Romeo's house as he sits watching telly in the front room with Sandra and his mum. *

KNOCKS (V.O.)
But I won't. I've aged, become dull with time.

135 INT. KNOCKS HOUSE. BEDROOM. NIGHT 13 135

We cut back to Knocks' room. He lies awake in bed writing in his book. We hear the last line of his story as he writes it.

KNOCKS (V.O.)
The dust has settled over my frame and no-one will wipe it away.

He turns out the light. We cut to black.

136 EXT. ROMEO'S HOUSE/STREET. NEXT MORNING. DAY 14 136

We fade up to a view of the two houses in the morning, the final morning of the film. We see Morell in his car a few houses away. He's obviously stayed the night, he appears to be in a bit of a state.

137 INT. ROMEO'S HOUSE. BEDROOM. - MORNING 14 137

We see Carol enter Romeo's room. He is asleep. She sits on his bed. She doesn't speak. After a short while Romeo sits up.

ROMEO
Ey'up.

CAROL
D'ya want me to get your dad to leave Romeo.

Romeo stays in silence and shrugs his shoulders

CONTINUED

137 CONTINUED: 137

CAROL
(continuing)
We can't all go on like this duckie. I don't want you keep going up his flat Romeo.

ROMEO
I 'm not going to.

We see a tenderness and understanding in Carol in this scene. She can tell that Romeo is very unhappy. We can feel her warmth as she speaks to Romeo.

CAROL
D'ya promise me.Yeah

CAROL
(continuing)
Are you gonna go school.

ROMEO
One step at a time.

CAROL
Seriously though Romeo you can't just ignore your dad, Ladine wants him to be able to come round and stuff so think on ah... I'll go and make you some breakfast. What d'ya fancy.

ROMEO
Have we got any Beans and Sausauges..

CAROL
Yeah. How many toast.

ROMEO
Six please.

138 INT. KNOCKS HOUSE. KITCHEN. MORNING 14 138

Sandra is sat in the kitchen. Bill walks in through the back door.

BILL
A slept in the shed.

CONTINUED

138 CONTINUED: 138

SANDRA
And..

BILL
..You obviously haven't done much thinkin..Is he back here again then.

SANDRA
He's got to teach Gavin Bill.

BILL
We should try and get some bugger else.

139 EXT. ROMEO'S HOUSE. FRONT GARDEN. - MORNING 14 139

We see Romeo exit his house in his school uniform. He is heading off to school. We see him walk down the road. A little further down the road Morell spots him and gets out of the van. Romeo turns round to walk back to the house as soon as he spots him.

MORELL
Romeo, please, just listen to me. Something terrible has happened. Something awful.

Morell begins to cry.

140 INT. KNOCKS HOUSE. BEDROOM. MORNING 14 140

We see Knocks in bed. Mr Laws has a big box with him

MR LAWS
I've got a surprise for you Gavin..

KNOCKS
What is it..

MR LAWS
Open it and look..

Mr. Laws passes him the box.

MR. LAWS
It's from the school non uniform day.

CONTINUED

140 CONTINUED: 140

Knocks opens it. It is full of magic tricks and magic books. Knocks is pleased but doesn't seem over the moon. He begins to look over the tricks.

141 EXT. LADINE'S SHOP/STREET. MORNING 14 141

We cut to the two in the van, they pull up in their usual place opposite the shop. We cut into the van. The music is on quite loud. The two have not spoken since perhaps Morell picked him up earlier. Morell appears absolutely wrecked. His hair is all over the place and he begins to sprout tears from his eyes.

ROMEO
What's up with ya..

MORELL
Arrgg.. Oh God.

Romeo is surprised at Morell's condition, he smirks.

MORELL
(continuing)
Please don't man.. Oh God.. I ain't slept all night, Arr Jesus..

ROMEO
What is it..

MORELL
It's ya fuckin sister man.. She's with someone else man.. A saw them together last night.. Arrg a feel ill.. aar shit shit..

ROMEO
A don't know what to say..

They are silent.

ROMEO
(continuing)
A'm gonna have to get to school in a minute.

MORELL
Romeo, this is fuckin important mate.. Y'know what a mean.

CONTINUED

141 CONTINUED: 141

ROMEO
I can't come round anymore.

MORELL
Be there for me man.. That's all, A'm sufferin.. I've got bad things running around me head man. I might kill meself, ya know what a mean. A thought we'd be a couple an that Y'know.. A'd thought things through.. It's just like 'wham', Y'know.. A dunna know what I'll do Romeo man..

ROMEO
A've got to get to school Morell..

MORELL
It's like you and ya whole family man.. always in me fuckin head.. Y'know what a mean..

ROMEO
A've got to go..

MORELL
A can't believe you ya fuckin dick splat.. A've been there for you man.. All through ya old man an everythin.. One fuckin thing man.. One fuckin time.. And ya just fuckin fuck off.

ROMEO
What d'ya want from me..

MORELL
On the bible.. I'll kill meself Romeo..

142 INT. KNOCKS HOUSE. BEDROOM. MORNING 14 **142**

Knocks is in bed. Bill enters. He wakes his son and then gets the tray with toast and cereal from outside the door. He sits as Knocks eats.

BILL
You alright.

CONTINUED

142 CONTINUED: 142

KNOCKS
Yer..

BILL
You gettin many sores.

KNOCKS
A few..

BILL
A don't know ah..

That's the end of that chat. They are silent for a while. Knocks reaches for a can of pop. Bill helps, then lights his cigar.

KNOCKS
Can you not light that in here.

BILL
Sorry.

He goes to put it out in a can of pop.

KNOCKS
Not there..

Bill looks around for something to put it out on.

BILL
I'll put it down the loo.

The end of another great chat. Bill walks out to flush his cigar away. We cut back they are silent again for a moment.

BILL
(continuing)
I expect you heard what went on yesterday.

Knocks nods his head.

BILL
(continuing)
Well I just want you to know that I've decided not to leave. I couldn't do that lad. I'm not going now.

?

142 CONTINUED: (2) 142

KNOCKS
Really?

Knocks is being sarcastic.

143 EXT. LADINE'S SHOP (STREET). DAY 12 143

Morell and Romeo are in the van outside Ladine's shop. Romeo has made the mistake of listening to what Morell has to say.They are sat watching Darren smooching with Ladine over the counter.

MORELL
A can't believe it..

ROMEO
Maybe He's a friend Morell..

MORELL
He's fucking stroking her man....

Morell thumps the wheel and screams.

MORELL
(continuing)
Arr man, it makes me ill..

Romeo feels very uncomfortable.

ROMEO
Can i go please..

MORELL
A can't man.. Ya gonna have ta do somethin..

ROMEO
Like what..

MORELL
A don't know man.. Talk to her..
Or talk to him.. Somethin man..
It's fuckin horrible..
I'll be dead Romeo. If you don't help me. I'll be swinging from a tree this afternoon.A'm just gonna jump in the river Y'know what a mean..

CONTINUED

143 CONTINUED: 143

MORELL
(continuing)
Look, he's leavin man.. Go and tell him to stay away or somethin..

ROMEO
A can't do that.. A'm not bloody Clint Eastwood..

MORELL
A thought ya fuckin liked me man.. A thought ya cared..

ROMEO
A do..

MORELL
Well do this one thing for me man, for Christ's sake Y'know what a mean.. He won't do anythin, you're a kid man.. Just tell him to f off..

ROMEO
It won't work Morell..

He gets out of the van and crosses the street. Darren is seen to walk out of the shop at the same time. We stay with Morell. Romeo manages to stop Darren a few shops down from Jeans Jeans. We see them talk. Morell is building up into a bigger state than his previous one. He gets out of the van and walks across the street. We follow him. Ahead we see the two talking. The build up is drawn out. Morell's walk across the street seems to take forever. He has built up a head of steam by the time he arrives. His talking will become shouting during the following exchange.

MORELL
What ya pickin on him for.

DARREN
Y'what..

MORELL
He's only a kid man, what ya pickin on him for..

DARREN
A don't know what ya talkin about.

CONTINUED

143 CONTINUED: (2) 143

MORELL
Pick on me.. Go on pick on me..

DARREN
Look mate I don't...

MORELL
Pick on me ya little fuckin prick..

Morell pulls a short crowbar out of his coat and smacks Darren round the back of the neck Darren drops straight to the floor. Morell throws the bar down.

ROMEO
Morell, what ya do'in..

MORELL
Get up then ya beast..

Morell grabs a wheelie bin. As Darren stands, he starts to club him with it.

ROMEO
Get off him Morell..

Morell switches to hands and feet for more of this beating. He steps back, like the boxer watching the fallen fighter take the count.

MORELL
Come on.. Come on.. Fuckin get up then..

In he goes again, stamping on his face and kicking the wind from his lungs. Darren is screaming for Romeo to stop him. Morell kicks him in the face and knocks him unconscious.

ROMEO
Morell that's enough..

Romeo steps in trying to pull Morell off.

Turning on Romeo, he slaps him round the face with some force. Putting Romeo on his arse.

MORELL
Fuck off. Just fuck off..

ROMEO
Alright alright..

CONTINUED

143 CONTINUED: (3) 143

Romeo scrambles to get out of the way. Morell turns his attention back to Darren.

MORELL
Come on ya piece of shit..

He stands over him for a minute, then spits on his victim's blooded head.

MORELL
(continuing)
Let's go Romeo..

Romeo is totally shellshocked. He doesn't reply. He just looks at the man lying unconscious on the floor. There is a stream of blood coming from Darren's face.

MORELL
(continuing)
I didn't mean to smack you..

Again Romeo does not, cannot reply.

MORELL
(continuing)
Well fuckin, just fuck off then..

He walks away to his van. Romeo crouches over Darren, to check he's ok. He then runs off.

144 INT. KNOCKS HOUSE. BEDROOM. DAY 14 144

We cut to the following shot of Knocks in his room. He's asleep on his bed surrounded by one hundred pounds worth of magic tricks, from the school's no uniform day. A magical extravaganza: doves, rabbits, cups and balls, linking rings, red sponge balls, giant cards and a glamourous assistant..

145 EXT. KNOCKS HOUSE. BACK GARDEN. DAY 14 145

Romeo walks round to Knocks' house. He goes around the back and knocks on the door, no answer, he tries to open it but it's locked. He calls up to Knocks' room.

146 INT. KNOCKS HOUSE. BEDROOM. DAY 14 146

We cut inside, Knocks is fast asleep in his bed, with his writing book.

147 EXT. KNOCKS HOUSE. BACK DOOR. DAY 14 147

Romeo sits on the back step of the house. He's obviously been very shaken by the events of the day - hence chose to come here rather than home.

He begins to cry.

148 OMITTED 148 *

149 EXT. KNOCKS HOUSE. (SIDE PASSAGE/BACK DOOR). DAY 14 149

Bill and Sandra continue. They walk along the path and make their way to the back door. * *

BILL
Romeo..

Romeo looks up. He stands and tries to push himself past Bill. Bill stops him..

BILL
(continuing)
Ae.. ae.. hang on.. Come here..

(Stage direction omitted) *

BILL
(continuing)
..You Ok lad..

ROMEO
Yer, fine..

For the first time we see a warmth and gentle consideration in Bill that has always been lacking in his character.

BILL
You sure, do ya want me to get your mum..

Romeo is trying to stop himself from crying.,

ROMEO
I'm fine..

CONTINUED

149 CONTINUED: 149

BILL
What's go'in on Romeo..

ROMEO
Nothin.. Will you tell him I called..

Romeo goes to leave, Although Bill doesn't know exactly what's wrong with Romeo, he feels very bad and responsible for him.

BILL
Stay there, take ya time.. You want some water..

ROMEO
No thanks..

BILL
What's happened.. Is it this bloody Morell.

Romeo falls silent.

BILL
(continuing)
Our Gavin's been worried sick.. You want me to come round to yours with ya..

ROMEO
No.. I'll be alright..

BILL
You sure..

ROMEO
Yer..

150 INT. KNOCKS HOUSE. BEDROOM. DAY 14 150

We cut to Knocks in his room. He's also heard most of the conversation. He calls for his mum to find out what's going on.

151 EXT. ROMEO'S HOUSE/STREET. DAY 14 151

Morell pulls up in his van. Still in a complete mess. He climbs out and starts shouting for Romeo.

CONTINUED

151 CONTINUED: 151

He stands on the front garden looking into the house through the letter box and then lounge window.

MORELL
Romeo open the fuckin door man..
Romeo..I'm in trouble man.

152 EXT. KNOCKS HOUSE. BACK DOOR/FRONT GARDEN. DAY 14 152

Bill, Romeo and Sandra have all heard this. Romeo is ushered into the house. Bill heads off out front. We see Bill come down the path of his house and meet Morell at the front.

153 EXT. ROMEO'S HOUSE/STREET. DAY 14 153

Bill is stood on the pavement. Morell is standing by his van out of control. Mouthing off at him. Bill is trying to talk Morell down. Morell is listening to Bill but keeps rising and falling in his rage.

BILL
You'd better calm yourself down abit.

MORELL
What's it got to do with you, you silly old bastard.

BILL
Come on man. Just fucking leave it. I know all about you.
So unless you want the police involved you'd better just shove off.

MORELL
Do'ya want a smack in the mouth.

BILL
Don't come that with me, you can't push me around, you big bloody bully.

MORELL
Listen you fucking prick, I'm not here to see you. If you don't get back inside, I smack you round the back of the head with a fucking lump hammer.

CONTINUED

153 CONTINUED: 153

Bill goes quite. He is starting to loose it. He is shaking. A tear rolls down the side of his cheek.

MORELL
(continuing)
Are you crying Gill.

Bill's face has gone white. His face has gone from one of fear to one of cold rage. He does not respond to Morell's jeers, he justs stares him in the face.

MORELL
(continuing)
Go on then... Do summut then.. Am gonna hit you with my hammer now gill you grey maniac.

Morell goes to get the hammer from his van. Bill blows. He goes for Morell. Morell turns and screams at him.

MORELL
(continuing)
Come on then.

They start fighting. None of them get any clean punches in. Bill is overpowering him. They wrestle all over the road, screaming in rage. Bill manages to hold him on the floor.

He pulls his hand out and punches Morell, starts squealing, at that moment Joseph comes steaming round the corner in his van, with Ladine in a complete mess in the passenger seat. She has obviously found out about the previous fight. Joseph jumps out and runs straight over to the two men on the floor. Joseph winches Bill off Morell and then stands over Morell. Bill comes back at Morell.

JOESPH
That's enough Bill. Facking stop it.

Bill backs off breathing heavily. We see Carol run out of the front door.

JOESPH
(continuing)
Carol get Ladine in the house.

MORELL
Ladine. Ladine.

CONTINUED

153 CONTINUED: (2) 153

JOESPH
You ya piece of shit. You'd better get in your Van and fack off before I do somfin I'll regret.

We see Carol usher Ladine back towards the house.

MORELL
I'm a fuckin maniac man.

BILL
Go on piss off you scum bastard, piss off

Morell tries to get up off the floor. Joseph pushes him back down..

MORELL
I can't leave can I. Move back then. So I can get up.

Joseph steps back, Bill is still moving about like a lunatic. Morell cautiously gets to his feet and heads for his van. He gets in and starts the engine, there is a short pause. Eventually he drives off. Joseph and Bill are left standing in the middle of the road. We cut back into wide to reveal Sandra walking over to Bill. We see Carol standing looking out of their front room window.

Sandra puts her arm round Bill who is now crying his eyes out. Carol walks out of the front door and heads round to pick up Romeo. Joseph walks over and sits on the pavement.We hear the cello section from a song like 'Sad Lisa' by Cat Stevens.

154 INT. KNOCKS HOUSE. LOUNGE/FRONT DOOR. LATER THAT DAY 14154

We cut into the front room at Knocks' house. We see Carol and Ladine sat on the sofa. Bill is on his chair. Sandra walks through with a pot of tea and cups etc. on a large tray. The room is very silent. We have never seen this lot all together in the film. Although silent, the atmosphere is warm and relaxed. Nothing is said, the tea is poured, we follow this in real time. The camera paying attention to nuances of this ritual. The back door goes and Joesph enters the front room.

SANDRA
Joseph..

CONTINUED

MAGIC

154 CONTINUED: 154

JOSEPH
Milk and three please.

CAROL
Milk and Four please.

Sandra continues and passes the tea to Joseph and Carol. We cut upstairs.

155 INT. KNOCKS HOUSE. BEDROOM. DAY 14 155

Knocks is sat up in bed. Romeo is slumped on the opposite side of the room. Again, for a while there is a moment of warm silence as the music fades.

ROMEO
How much longer have you got..

KNOCKS
It depends... You know, it's difficult to tell.

ROMEO
I'll bring you a box of maltesers if you like..

KNOCKS
Whatever yeah... I'm gonna be a magician.

ROMEO
Are ya.

KNOCKS
I want too like.. That and Poetry.

Romeo spies the magic tricks down the side of the bed.

ROMEO
Is that the stuff the school bought you.

KNOCKS
Yeah. It's semi professional.

ROMEO
Really..

CONTINUED

155 CONTINUED: 155

KNOCKS
My dads gonna build me a stand for it all.

There is a long pause.

ROMEO
I'll come round after school tomorrow if you like and you can show me some tricks and that.

KNOCKS
Erm... I'll have to ask my mum, but it should be alright I think. I can't promise that I'll need an assitant though. You might just be a helper.

ROMEO
All the best magicians have assistants though.

156 EXT. KNOCKS' BACK GARDEN. END CREDITS. DAY 15 156 *

We begin on the hillside, where the film began, with Knocks and Romeo practising their newly formed magic act.

Knocks the Magician, dressed in his grandad's enormous black trench coat, Romeo, Maggie the Assistant, with blacked out teeth and loads of egg and cress sandwiches stuffed down his/her tights. We see their offbeat rehearsal unfold as though we, the camera, were the audience. Alongside the music we dissolve from the magic wand into their rehearsed trick where we cut away to an overhead shot rotating and rising until fading to black. The music continues for the end titles.

157 EXT TOY BUS - DAY 157 *

(Scene to be written) *

158 EXT TOY BUS - DAY 158 *

(Scene to be written) *

THE END

CAST

Romeo Brass	Andrew Shim
Gavin(Knocks) Wooley	Ben Marshall
Morell	Paddy Considine
Steven Laws	Bob Hoskins
Joseph Brass	Frank Harper
Carol Brass	Ladene Hall
Ladine Brass	Vicky Mclure
Bill Woolley	James Higgins
Sandra Woolley	Julia Ford
Dennis Wardrobe	Martin Arrowsmith
School Pianist	Dave Blant
Darren	Darren Campbell
Physiotherapist	Paul Fraser
Neighbour Lad#2	Nicholas Harvey
Fish & Chip Shop Man	Shane Meadows
Park Lad #1	Joel Morris
Clifford	Johann Myers
Headmistress	Tanya Myers
Ambulance Man	Sammi Pasha
Neighbour Lad #1	Jamahl Peterkin
Park Lad #2	James Tomlinson

CREW

Director	Shane Meadows
Writers	Shane Meadows
	Paul Fraser
Producers	George Faber
	Charlie Pattinson
Executive Producers	Andras Hamori
	David Thompson
Story Editor	Robyn Slovo
Line Producer	Ronaldo Vasconcellos
Director of Photography	Ashley Rowe
Production Designer	Crispian Sallis
Film Editor	Paul Tothill
Supervising Sound Editor	Catherine Hodgson
Dubbing Mixer	Paul Hamblin
Sound Recordist	Colin Nicholson
Costume Designer	Robin Fraser Paye
Hair & Make-up Design	Pebbles
Casting Director	Abi Cohen